Praise for Geoff Symon

"If you haven't heard Geoff Symon's class on forensics and crime scene investigation, hurry. Fascinating, weirdly fun and totally accessible. A must for crime and suspense writers."
– Kristan Higgins, *New York Times*, *USA TODAY*, *Wall Street Journal* and *Publishers Weekly* bestselling author

"Shout out to Geoff Symon, whose forensic advice is helping to make my current work in progress bloody believable."
– Christopher Rice, *New York Times* bestselling author

"When I have to write forensics scenes in my stories, my go-to source to get all the details right is Geoff Symon. His first-hand experience, as well as his ability to explain the world of crime scene investigations, have been invaluable resources. It's been a mystery to me why Geoff hasn't been writing this down. Now, thankfully, he is."
– Ron Marz, award winning comic book and graphic novel author

Crime Scenes

Forensics for Fiction Series

by Geoff Symon

Published by Evil Mastermind, LLC
New York, NY
EvilMastermind.com
First Publication: 22 March 2017

Edited by Erin O'Brien
Illustrations by Evil Mastermind, LLC
Book formatting by BB eBooks

ISBN 978-1-945043-12-3 (Ebook)
ISBN 978-1-945043-13-0 (Print)

Website: www.ForensicsForFiction.com

To the authors whose scenes in their books
are the scenes of their crimes.

Contents

Acknowledgements

There are so many wonderful people who participated in this project. Many thanks to Robin Covington and Sara Humphreys who gave up their time and readily provided needed input.

Special thanks to Pamela Burford, whose eye for detail smoothed out many a bump in this road.

A hearty shout-out to Regina Kyle and Terence Keenan, who allowed me to exploit their expertise in their careers which strengthened my content – Thank you.

A badge of honor needs to go to Kate McMurray, who was able to stitch together my word salad and fine-tuned it into a product I'm beyond proud of.

And, of course, thank you to my partner in crime, who never rests, never settles, and never lacks as inspiration.

Preface

When I taught forensics studies at the George Washington University in Washington, DC, and Marymount University in Maryland, I was amazed at my dedicated and enthusiastic students. As an adjunct professor, I first fully grasped how much interest exists for a career field to which I've dedicated twenty years.

I live with a successful author. Three years ago various writing groups and conventions began inviting me to present forensic courses at their gatherings. Authors turned out to be even hungrier for realism than I'd expected. They might deal in make-believe, but they wanted their stories anchored in truth.

All the different writer audiences made one thing clear: few reference books hit the sweet spot between minutiae and fluff. While many books exist on crimes and investigative techniques, very few address the unique challenges of writing genre fiction.

That need gave birth to the *Forensics for Fiction Series*. In these books, I'm distilling all of my training and experience as a twenty-year forensic investigator and my personal involvement with the genre community. Each book will provide a targeted overview of a different aspect of criminal investigations. I'll present each topic as a heaping platter of research goodies for writers of every genre to choose from, depending on what works for the story in front of them.

I want this book to be accessible and helpful, so rather than bury you under a wall of impenetrable text, I've broken up each chapter with insets:

- *PROCEDURES* and *TERMS*: highlighting how real-life law enforcement officials operate and actual language they use.
- *ACCURACY* and *PITFALLS*: providing practical tips to steer authors away from common errors.
- *FUN FACTS*: sharing entertaining tidbits to spark an idea or inspire a plot bunny.
- *ALERTS*: identifying specialized sections that may only interest exhaustive researchers. Whenever you see the Alert symbol—

—I am letting you know that the following section may be more technical than your book requires. If you don't need to know the physics and math involved, feel free to skip these marked sections. You can pick up at the next section seamlessly.

I make sure to provide plenty of illustrations to clarify and drive home every concept. Additionally, I include true-crime case studies relevant to the topic and talk about my own investigations.

I hope you find this book informative and entertaining, but mostly hope you find it useful in your next great story.

Chapter 1: Introduction and Legal Concepts

"The game is afoot!"

– The Adventures of the Abbey Grange
by Sir Arthur Conan Doyle

In the above quote, Sherlock Holmes sums up the urgency of a criminal investigation perfectly. With things already "afoot," Holmes and Watson have no time to waste. Holmes recognized every crime includes a ticking clock, because the more time that passes, the "colder" the case gets. Evidence can deteriorate, be covered up, misplaced, or destroyed. Memory details can get cloudy or altogether forgotten. Holmes understood a fundamental principle to investigating crimes: the quicker he responds to the crime scene, the more conspicuous the evidence.

The purpose of *Crime Scenes: Forensics for Fiction Series* is to provide writers with a well-rounded understanding of crime scenes, including their components, their participants, and their rules and procedures. Naturally, I feel all areas of this book are important to this discussion, yet some topics may tend to get a bit more technical than you, the author writing a crime scene, need (or want!) for your story. I will endeavor to keep this topic fun and accessible and always give you a shortcut to skip sections that may not apply to you or your plot. Although why anyone would want to skip fun and accessible Symon rantings is beyond me!

Before we get into the down and dirty of crime scenes themselves, there are a few basic concepts we need to establish first. In order to prove that Kate committed the crime, investigators must show that Kate was at the scene. This is called the **linkage theory**: the idea that the suspect must be connected to the victim and/or the scene. The linkage theory does not solve the crime, because it is not proof, it simply associates two major components of the event. For example, Kate is linked to the murder site because the victim died in her apartment. However, just because Kate is connected to the scene by living there, this link does not prove Kate killed the victim. The linkage theory becomes important when Kate cannot be connected to the scene. If the murder happened in Moscow, and Kate had never been to Russia before, her involvement becomes highly questionable.

Crimes are solved through evidence, which is the proof I touched on above. Evidence either proves or disproves how a crime was committed and/or who participated in it. There are three categories of

evidence: **testimonial, documentary,** and **physical.**
Testimonial evidence is an interview. Documentary evidence is informational evidence, such as financial information on tax returns, the video footage from a security camera, or the contents of a suicide note. Physical evidence is everything else. So, to make the distinction, if the writing on the paper is what's significant, that is counted as documentary evidence. When a suicide note reads that all of the deceased's possessions will be inherited by Bob, the gardener, investigators consider that information as important, and take it as documentary evidence. However, if the actual, tangible piece of paper is what is important to the case, then it is physical evidence. When a detective discovers the stationery used for the note is very specific paper, only made by one company and only sold to Her Majesty, the Queen of England, that paper is physical evidence. The vast majority of evidence collected for a case is physical evidence.

Investigators look for evidence at the **crime scene,** which is any place associated with the alleged crime. These locales can be where the crime was committed, where it was planned, any vehicle used for transportation, or any place evidence was disposed of. To put simply, the purpose of crime scene searches is to identify and collect evidence.

> **TERMS** – A crime scene is any locale associated in any way with a criminal act where evidence may exist. Remember, the evidence proves or disproves how the crime occurred and who was involved.

Edmond Locard, a forensics pioneer from the early 1900s, wrote extensively on the importance of evidence. He promoted an idea that later became known as **Locard's Exchange Principle**, also called Locard's Theory of Exchange and Locard's Theory of Interchange. Locard theorized that whenever two objects come into contact, an exchange occurs. Forensically, he postulated that whenever a crime is committed, the suspect leaves something of himself at the scene, such as a fingerprint, hair, or footprint, and takes part of the scene with him, such as a shard of broken glass, pet hair, or carpet fibers. These exchanged items are the evidence investigators are seeking when they set up a crime scene.

Locard's Exchange Principle does not stop at the commission of the crime, however. Every living being on that scene afterward, be it an animal, the person who discovered the scene, or the police officers who process it, change it by leaving part of themselves and taking part of it away.

FUN FACT – Many a police procedural use Locard's Exchange Principle to inspire dramatic complications, because everyone on a crime scene, whether villain or hero, interacts with it.

Using Locard's Exchange Principle in conjunction with the linkage theory, the evidence forms the **evidence triangle**, which shows how the evidence links the scene to the suspect, the suspect to the victim, and the victim to the scene. Investigators' goals are to establish those connections as proof, clarifying what happened. That is why crime scenes become so important. Sloppy crime scenes make for weak evidence links, or evidence missed altogether.

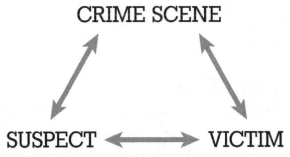

Figure 1: Evidence Triangle

Since the purpose of establishing a crime scene is to locate the evidence and create the evidence triangle, at this point in the introduction we need to discuss the laws that regulate those searches. Before I do, however, I want to acknowledge that I am exceedingly grateful for my international readers. I must point out that while the essence of processing crime scenes and identifying evidence resonates globally, the specific laws governing law enforcement agencies may differ country to country. If you are from a nation other than the United States, or are writing a law enforcement character from a different country, please verify how different specific laws and procedures apply to that region. All of my experience is in dealing with the American system, and that's the basis of the material that follows.

> ALERT – The following section becomes more technical than most writers need for their stories. It covers the laws of the United States that regulate American crime scene processing and explains the origins of those controls. Those needing just the essentials of crime scenes can skip ahead to the next section titled "Legal Searches."

Constitutional Law

If the purpose of establishing a crime scene is to search for evidence, then the laws applied to it grant or limit the authority to conduct that search. When the Founding Fathers of the United States wrote the Constitution, literally writing America into existence, they faced significant resistance. Essentially, their newly established government had unchecked power, which was precisely what the Revolutionary War fought against.

James Madison spearheaded the movement to

amend the as–yet-unratified Constitution in order to address this imbalance, and drafted several articles. These articles were added to, combined, and adjusted until ultimately twelve were submitted for Congressional consideration. Ten of these articles became the first official Constitutional Amendments, and are now referred to as the Bill of Rights. All of these amendments provide private citizens with safeguards against governmental overreach.

The Fourth Amendment to the Constitution is the one that applies to the topic of crime scenes, as it addresses government searches. It reads as follows:

"The right of the people to be secure in their persons, houses, papers, and effects, against unreasonable searches and seizure, shall not be violated, and no warrants shall issue, but upon probable cause, supported by oath or affirmation, and particularly describing the place to be searched, and the persons or things to be seized."

Essentially, although the US Constitution does not explicitly state the phrase, this amendment provides for the right to privacy. Fundamentally, the Fourth Amendment protects private citizens from unwarranted searches by the government. That is why the legal document (officially called a writ) granting law enforcement the authority to search an area is called a "warrant." It shows why the situation *warrants* a law enforcement search.

Remember that the Bill of Rights applies to governmental actions, so the Fourth Amendment does not pertain to circumstances between citizens, such as a thief committing a home invasion. Other laws cover those situations.

> FUN FACT – Although the US Constitution does not specifically use the words "right to privacy," the Supreme Court has found that right to be implicit in the Fourth Amendment and have cited it in their decisions.

Let's break down the Fourth Amendment as it relates to crime scenes.

Where can law enforcement legally go? Like the other amendments, the Fourth Amendment was ratified as a means of protecting American citizens. This means the amendment limits the power of the government. Basically, it's telling the government what it *can't* do. Since this amendment establishes that citizens have a right to privacy, the government cannot simply concoct a crime scene and take citizens' property as evidence on a whim. This applies to every situation where a citizen should have privacy, or in other words, where privacy *was expected* by the citizen. This is where we get the legal concept of an **"expectation of privacy."**

Although the US Constitution sets up protections for American citizens, those rules are not all encompassing. They are enforced via a **reasonable** standard.

That is why the expectation of privacy does not apply to a public park. A reasonable person cannot walk around the park in a thong and expect not to be noticed. A reasonable person would have no *expectation* that his walk would be *private*. That same reasonable person, however, can expect to walk around inside his home without being watched.

> **TERMS – The reasonable standard is a legal determination that assesses what a prudent, informed person would likely expect or how that person would likely act given different circumstances.**

Applying the reasonable standard to the expectation of privacy generally means that a person's privacy extends to her body, clothing, personal belongings, and living area. For homeowners, the living area includes all owned property, including the house, the land surrounding the house, and any additional buildings on that land. In the suburbs, it's essentially the yard to the curb. For farms it can be all of the owned land if it is properly marked or closed off. The legal term for this area around the home is called the **curtilage**, and law enforcement may not search it without permission.

Vehicles and businesses also carry an expectation of privacy; however, the expectation is not as high as for a residence. Abandoned property does not have any Fourth Amendment protection, although law enforcement must prove it is indeed abandoned.

> **TERMS** – Curtilage is the area of land surrounding a dwelling that normally cannot be searched without explicit consent or a warrant.

It is important to point out that the Bill of Rights protects citizens from the <u>federal</u> government, and originally did not apply to state and local government workers. Does this mean your local police force is not bound by the laws of the Constitution? Can they search your property whenever they feel like it? No. The reason for that is the Fourteenth Amendment, which addresses citizenship rights and equal protection under the law. Under its Due Process Clause, state and local officials are just as accountable to the Bill of Rights as their federal counterparts.

Legal Searches

So when can a search occur? Shows like *CSI* and *Law & Order* portray investigators doing searches all the time, so it must be possible. And it is, often. Remember, the Fourth Amendment protects our right to privacy, so anytime a crime scene needs to be searched in a public space or abandoned building, law enforcement can do their thing unimpeded. Only in situations where privacy is a factor does the legal system prevent investigators from searching an area, unless they take additional steps.

The surest standing law enforcement has when conducting a search in a private area is when they obtain a **search warrant**. As stated previously, a warrant is a legal document, issued by a judge or magistrate, granting the officer permission to enter and search that area.

There are strict rules governing warrants. First, the presenting officer must prove that a warrant is necessary. Judges will err on the side of the citizen, so the investigator must build a case to prove why this situation requires this particular search. In other words, the investigator must make clear to the judge that there is probable cause to believe evidence will be found in the area identified.

Probable cause means investigators have current, reliable information that strongly suggests there is evidence in the area to be searched. The police cannot search anywhere solely because an investigation is open. Therefore, requesting a search of a house because someone went to school with the victim when they were in third grade is not probable cause that evidence will be in there. Likewise, asking for a warrant because someone was once convicted of a similar crime is not probable cause that he was involved this time. However, when a person reports his Rolex was stolen from his gym locker and his workout partner posted pictures on Facebook showing himself wearing a similar watch he previously did not own, investigators have probable cause to believe the watch may be in his home. The probable cause requirement is such a high standard because its purpose is to protect citizens from extreme or excessive use of law enforcement authority.

> TERMS – Probable cause is a level of certainty required from a law enforcement official in order to convince a judge or magistrate to grant a search warrant for a private area.

Search warrants are also incredibly specific. Law enforcement agents may only search the specific listed area and only for the items explicitly spelled out in the document. A search warrant does not provide a free pass for law enforcement. On the contrary, it is extremely limiting.

- If a search warrant has an error and lists the address of the next door residence instead of the suspect's residence, law enforcement must correct the error prior to entering the suspect's home.
- If the warrant allows the search of "Doctors Medical Group, Inc." files, investigators cannot open "Surgeons R Us Medical Services" boxes that may be stored in the same warehouse.
- If the warrant allows the search of a residence for stolen jewelry, police do not have permission to go through the suspect's phone.

- If the warrant allows investigators to search for an eighty-eight-inch HDTV believed to be hidden in the home, agents cannot go through the suspect's desk, because no TV that size would fit in the drawers. In most cases, law enforcement tries to get permission for the smallest items possible so they can search the entire premises.

Legal Search Exceptions

Unfortunately, life has a way of throwing gray areas into the clear-cut rules we set up for ourselves. Naturally, circumstances arise where a warrantless search does not violate the Constitution. These situations fall into the following exceptions:

- <u>Consent</u>. If someone agrees to have their person or premises searched, no search warrant is required.
  - The person must give the consent voluntarily and the consent may be revoked at any time.
  - If another person has their own legitimate access to the area, that person can give consent for the search instead of the suspect.
    - In a roommate situation, the roommate can only give consent to the common areas of the dwelling (kitchen, living

room, etc.) but may not give consent to the suspect's bedroom.

- Even if the keys to the suspect's car are in a common area, that does not mean the roommate can give consent to search that vehicle.

- <u>Plain View</u>. As long as the law enforcement official is legally allowed to be in the spot he's standing in, if something illegal is in obvious sight, he does not need a warrant to enter that area.

  ○ If the police are given consent by a roommate to search the living room, but through the suspect's open bedroom door they see uncut sheets of counterfeit money, they may now enter the room for the purpose of seizing that evidence, even if the reason they were in the house had nothing to do with counterfeiting.

  ○ Plain smell and plain sound apply as well. In most jurisdictions, if a police officer lawfully pulls a vehicle over, and during that stop smells marijuana, he can search that vehicle for the contraband without a warrant. As I mentioned before, however, a residence has a much higher expectation of privacy than a vehicle does, and many jurisdiction do not allow plain smell to be the sole reason for a warrantless search of a home.

- <u>Execution of an Arrest Warrant</u>. During a lawful arrest, the arresting official may search the arrested person's body and immediate surroundings without a search warrant.
- <u>Prevention of Evidence Destruction</u>. If there is a reasonable and true indication that in the time required to obtain a valid search warrant evidence will be destroyed, law enforcement officers may enter a premises for the purpose of preventing that destruction. Cops are held to a very high standard, and must prove their belief the evidence will be removed or destroyed is valid. Simply concluding that "if it were me, I'd flush the drugs" is not a legitimate reason to act. The police officers have no reasonable indication the suspects would do this action before they got a search warrant. However, if the cops detain a suspect outside, and he yells, "Flush it, Marsha, flush it all!" and then they hear repeated toilet flushing, this exception becomes reasonable. If cops abuse this exception, not only do they face personal or professional repercussions, but, as we'll cover in the next section, any evidence they obtain in this or later related searches cannot be considered in any court proceedings.

- <u>Ensuring the Safety of Others</u>. Whenever a person's life or health is at risk, investigators are expected to act immediately to save them. This is the permission police use to enter a residence when someone reports they haven't heard from the owner. Likewise, if the police respond to a neighbor's noise complaint and hear screaming inside, they are allowed to forcefully enter.

Legal Punishments for Illegal Searches

So why should law enforcement care about the rules? If they enforce the law, shouldn't they be able to get away with whatever they want?

The American legal system put two doctrines into place to ensure that wasn't the case. These punishments target the outcomes of illegal searches—the evidence collected—as a way of deterring the police from abusing their power. The **Exclusionary Rule** tackles exactly that: any evidence collected during an illegal search is inadmissible at trial. Anything associated with that search cannot be used to prove the investigator's case. The court treats it as if it never existed. The only reason to do an illegal search is to gain evidence more easily or to target a specific person, so because the legal system makes that evidence inadmissible, breaking the search and seizure rules becomes counterproductive for law enforcement and takes away any benefit.

- If an officer enters the home of a habitual drug user without a warrant and with no legal search exceptions, no drugs found during that search can be used against the user, ever.

- If an investigator gains access to an apartment by a roommate's consent, but then illegally enters and searches the suspect's bedroom, everything found during that search is inadmissible to any legal proceeding.

- If a cop tries to claim he was preventing the destruction of evidence, but he cannot adequately prove the reasonableness of his position, nothing he "saved" will be considered as evidence.

However, a particularly savvy investigator may rationalize that sacrificing the seized evidence would be worth the information gained during the illegal search, especially if that information led to the solving of his case. So a second doctrine was enacted to counter this "breaking the law for the greater good" mentality.

The **Fruit of the Poisonous Tree** doctrine establishes that not only is that initial evidence collected at the scene inadmissible at trial based on the Exclusionary Rule, but so is anything obtained down the line as a result of that search. In the court's eyes, not only is the initial evidence tainted by the illegal search, but so is every lead developed from that search, which then taints any search (even if done appropriately) derived from those leads, and so on. Everything that results from an illegal search, no matter how much later in the investigation, and regardless of how significant to the outcome, is kept from any sort of prosecution, essentially negating the entire case.

- During an illegal search for stolen art, an officer finds insurance paperwork for a car he did not previously know about. Weeks later he discovers that car at a person's house he did not know was involved in the theft. Even if he obtains a search warrant and *legally* searches this new suspect's house, where he finds the paintings, none of that can be used in his case, because he was pointed in that direction from the illegal search.

- If an investigator in a Ponzi scheme case enters a person's curtilage without a warrant to go through the trash, meaning the bins have not been put on the street yet, and finds several discarded copies of a ransom note for an unrelated kidnapping investigation, any evidence found in searches made based solely on the note will not be considered.

Jurisdiction

The final legal concept I want to cover is that of **jurisdiction**, which assigns the legal authority in an investigation. Sometimes jurisdiction depends on geographical territory, sometimes on the agency, and sometimes on the type of crime. Essentially, when related to crime scenes, jurisdiction determines which agency will run the case, which in itself determines who is allowed to be at the crime scene.

Many different law enforcement jurisdictions cover the United States. Local territories like towns and cities have police, counties have sheriffs, states have state police, and the feds have a host of agencies with special agents, including the Federal Bureau of Investigation (FBI), the Central Intelligence Agency (CIA), the US Secret Service (USSS), and many, many others. The level of government that has jurisdiction over the crime scene determines who has authority there and how far it extends.

You'll see a great example of how jurisdiction affects who is in charge when you get to my case study of JonBenét Ramsey. In that particular case, jurisdiction fell to the FBI when it was first considered a kidnapping, but quickly reverted to the local police department when they discovered they were actually dealing with a murder.

Jurisdictional determination is a topic that goes much deeper than this book could cover in a reasonable space. For simplicity's sake, think of matters affecting the United States as a whole as *federal* jurisdiction while those affecting a person or single entity as *local* jurisdiction. The police tend to handle a murder, but the federal government takes cases involving terrorism or international affairs. No state has jurisdiction over any other state; therefore, the federal government also takes cases involving multiple states, such as drug trafficking, kidnappings, or a murder spree crossing state lines.

The Law and Your Story

What does all of this off-page background legalese mean when it comes to your story? It applies every time you want a character to roll out the crime scene tape. Where it becomes important to your story is in addressing why your character shows up in the first place. You have to answer two questions for every crime scene you write:

- Is my character there legally, or is she violating anyone's Fourth Amendment rights? Take the time to determine if she is searching in a public space. If not, does she have a warrant? If not, which of the legal search exceptions is she enacting? If none of these apply, are you going to address any consequences of the illegal search?
- Does my character have jurisdiction in this case, or does she have to hand over the reins to another agency? Decide what town/city your crime is committed in and then do a little

research to determine if your character's agency has the correct authority to investigate it.

Once these two questions are answered, you can begin to process your fictional scene with confidence. As we begin the discussion of the crime scene itself, we need to identify who's there. From first responders to the search team, you have a lot of people to consider.

Chapter 2: First Responders

Now that we've established the legal framework for criminal investigators, let's focus on the crime scene itself. I will cover how to establish a crime scene and who is present. The initial response to a crime scene is very important, and law enforcement's primary goal is the preservation of evidence. However, there are other essential emergency personnel on the scene whose focus extends beyond evidence.

Types of Scenes

As the name suggests, the major component of creating a *crime* scene is the commission of a crime. So investigators establish crime scenes either as a result of leads they developed during the course of a criminal investigation or as an emergency response to the initial reporting/discovery of a criminal act.

Routine crime scenes are those initiated by investigators based on their active casework. We touched on these crime scenes previously. The investigators establish probable cause through the development of leads that demonstrate evidence exists at a specific location. They then follow the appropriate procedures to present their findings to a judge and obtain a search warrant.

> **PROCEDURE** – Without any sort of applicable exception, such as consent, officers must obtain a search warrant to enter any area with an established expectation of privacy.

An **emergency crime scene**, however, is for a crime that is reported prior to the initiation of an investigation. In this situation, the crime has either just occurred or was just discovered and emergency personnel are required. The alleged crime can be reported to a police officer on the street, by calling the local law enforcement agency or, as is most common with serious crimes, by calling 911. These scenes require emergency personnel to respond to a call. Think of an emergency crime scene as a response to an external notification and as the start of a case, while a routine crime scene is one developed internally by following leads during the course of an already active investigation.

Routine and emergency crime scenes are processed using the same strategies and tactics, which I'll cover in the next chapter. However, emergency crime scenes differ a bit because they normally do not require a search warrant for a variety of the exceptions we discussed in the last chapter (consent, prevention of evidence destruction, and ensuring the safety of others). They also involve emergency personnel, who are not normally required during a routine crime scene search. This chapter focuses on those emergency professionals and what their duties are at the crime scene.

Emergency Personnel

When a call comes in, 911 operators alert the appropriate response teams. They are trained to get as much information as possible and to keep the caller on the phone so that errors can be corrected easily and further developments can be reported immediately. Depending on the emergency, the 911 operators alert the applicable dispatchers to get the appropriate emergency response teams to the scene. These emergency response teams are called first responders.

First responders are police officers, firefighters, and emergency medical technicians (EMTs). All or some of these responders may be sent out, depending on the situation reported. Their jobs are to assess the situation, save human life, protect anyone from injury, protect property, and secure the evidence in the scene, in that order of priority. Therefore, the firefighters' and EMTs' duties will always take precedence over those of the cops.

TERMS – First responders are the initial professionals dispatched to the scene after an emergency is reported. They consist of the responding police officers, firefighters, and EMTs.

For the most part, firefighters and EMTs are separate entities. The firefighters respond from their firehouse and the EMTs from the hospital. However, in many cities and municipalities, firefighters are also trained to take on the EMT role. Even if the emergency does not include reports of fire, these firefighters are the ones to respond for medical assistance. They are fully certified EMTs. Should specialized medical care be needed, they then contact the hospital, and paramedics are sent out for patient transportation. As with every aspect of writing, each author should research the first responder setup for the setting of their story to determine who should be at their scene and what their responsibilities are.

Locard's Exchange Principle tells us that every person who enters a crime scene changes it. First responders are no exception. They may establish a crime scene, and they may protect it, but even they affect it. The question is, what changes can they avoid and what changes must they allow?

Evidence may be high on the police officer's mind, but even if there's risk of it being washed away by a firefighter's hose or trampled and otherwise compromised by an EMT's lifesaving acts, law enforcement officials will not interfere in those efforts. Public safety and human life are always more important.

- Police cannot delay firefighters from putting

out a fire in order to quickly identify and collect evidence that will most likely be destroyed by the water.

- EMTs will immediately enter a residence with as much equipment as they need to attempt to save a life. Police cannot interfere and try to save blood spatter, shoe prints, or any other evidence that may be in their way.
- The bomb squad will safely detonate an explosive device rather than trying to preserve any fingerprints on it.

Typically, the police are the first to arrive on the scene. Every action they take is first for safety and second for security. They begin assessing the situation immediately. They attempt to determine the validity of the call, gauge the imminent danger to those present, identify any injured persons, and secure the scene against tampering (purposeful or unintentional) by any suspect, witness, curious bystander, or passerby.

If medical treatment is necessary and the injured person is mobile, they attempt to move that person to an area away from the main scene to protect any evidence present. However, if the police cannot make a reasonable assertion that the injured person can move on his own, they do not have the authority to move him. The police cannot make medical assessments and cannot risk making an injury worse by

CRIME SCENES (FORENSICS FOR FICTION SERIES)

relocating the victim.

If a person's injuries are so severe that they are either incapacitated or presumed dead, the police will determine a pathway to and from the victim that is as direct as possible for medical personnel yet does not pose any threat to obvious evidence. Again, human life and well-being trump any evidence, and if the pathway cannot be easily routed around the evidence, and that evidence is not quickly collected, the EMTs will need to go through it to attend to the victim. No evidence is more important than human life.

> **PROCEDURE –** No evidence is important enough to slow down or inconvenience firefighters or medical personnel who are doing their job.

If law enforcement personnel determine a suspect is still present at the scene, and that person appears belligerent or dangerous, the suspect becomes the police officer's top priority. Safety of victims, witnesses, and fellow first responders is paramount so the situation does not worsen. Further, the security of the scene when dealing with suspects is also at risk. The responding police need to keep all suspects under control so they do not have the opportunity to destroy, hide, or change potential evidence.

If a suspect requires immediate serious medical attention, the EMTs or responding paramedics will transport the suspect to a hospital. Police officers will accompany the suspect and have him in custody at all times. The officers' primary duty is to let the medical personnel do their job, so they stay out of the way. At times law enforcement will be allowed in the room during medical procedures, but other times they will be ordered to stand outside. Any arrest or processing of the suspect happens after he is released from the hospital.

Even with all of these duties going on, the responding police officers at the crime scene also have the responsibility of taking note of everything they can:

- Who is present and why?
- What cars are present or left soon after the police arrived?
- What seems odd or suspicious?

These first responders will be the first people interviewed when the lead investigator arrives, and their training will make their observations highly significant.

Perimeter

After these initial steps are performed, the police officers' main efforts turn to securing the scene against any sort of alteration or contamination. This is called maintaining scene integrity.

Police achieve scene integrity through scene security. Officers make sure all witnesses, potential suspects, and victims are moved off of the scene and then establish a perimeter to prevent anyone from entering the scene without permission.

> **PROCEDURE –** Keeping scene integrity means striving to keep the scene in pristine condition.

The perimeter is typically made with yellow crime scene tape. The verbiage on the tape can vary from police department to police department, but most often reads "Crime Scene Do Not Cross," "Police Line Do Not Cross" or something similar.

Figure 2: Crime Scene Tape

The establishment of this perimeter becomes very important because if it is not out far enough, any evidence found outside of the marked, secured area can later come into question. For this reason, the police will try to *overestimate* how large a crime scene should be. A crime scene can always be made smaller, but rarely made larger.

In urban settings, the perimeter is often limited by environmental factors such as buildings, but generally the perimeter should be set out far enough so that a significant amount of space entirely surrounds the area of the crime scene. This perimeter's purpose is to keep unwanted persons off of the scene. Therefore the tape needs to be far enough out that the civilians attracted by the spectacle of police activity cannot in any way hinder the investigators doing their job or affect any potential evidence on the scene.

Of course, practical considerations need to be acknowledged as well. The farther out police push the perimeter, the more ground they have to patrol and protect against line jumpers. Also, the larger the overall scene, the greater the potential for disrupting those not involved with the case. For example, in a residential neighborhood, the farther out the perimeter is pushed, the greater the number of families who cannot get to their homes. The scene needs to be pushed out as far as possible without becoming a civil hindrance.

> ACCURACY – Civil hindrance is a real concern when establishing a crime scene. Rarely will an entire neighborhood be cordoned off.

Each crime scene has too many variables to simply state what distance is far enough out when establishing the perimeter. Many scenes require the police to account for enough room to create a second, inner perimeter. The outer perimeter prevents any unauthorized person from entering the scene while the inner perimeter creates an area where authorized personnel can gather, set up equipment and process evidence that is protected, without being on the target scene itself. We'll discuss these different areas and everything that goes on within the outer perimeter in the next chapter.

ACCURACY – A crime scene always has security. Stories involving a kooky show-up or an on-the-scene confrontation with members of the media, passersby, or rivals are unrealistic and often ridiculous.

The media tends to be a problem for crime scene investigators. News stories can potentially reveal case details to the public at large that law enforcement may prefer to keep from the perpetrator. While first responders never have authority to speak to the press, their establishment of the crime scene perimeter keeps the media out of the crime scene and away from any "scoop" not provided by the police department's public relations division. This is another reason law enforcement brass encourage the responding police to err on the side of making the secured scene overly large, assuming the civil hindrance issues are tolerable.

The police will set up a single entry/exit point at the perimeter. Everyone will have to pass through this point to get on or off the scene. This produces a measure of control and limits who can come onto the scene. It also allows the police to establish a log documenting everyone who entered the scene. An assigned officer maintains this entry/exit point log throughout the entire process, manning the entrance/exit point at all times until the scene is released.

> PROCEDURE – Logs become critical during the crime scene process. Entry/exit, evidence, and photo logs establish clarity and transparency.

As soon as the investigators arrive, control of the scene shifts to them, and they will begin the process of evaluating and searching the scene for evidence.

Once the first responder police have established and protected the scene, the lead investigator may use them as initial interviewers and canvassers. They are a ready resource that can do the initial interviews of the crowd, neighbors, and any possible witnesses. By conducting these interviews, the police take a massive task off of the investigators' shoulders and allow them to identify which potentially significant interviews they should follow-up on.

First responders both protect and contaminate a scene. They both create and change it. Their jobs, while at times risking the destruction of evidence, cannot be spoken of highly enough. They are essential, brave, dedicated women and men charged with impossible tasks, and I encourage a hearty "thank you" whenever you are presented the chance.

Now that the crime scene has been established, the next step is to process it.

Chapter 3: Crime Scene Processing

Once the investigators arrive at the crime scene, they assume control of it. One main investigator takes charge and follows a very methodical course of processing.

The Lead Investigator

For crime scenes in already opened, ongoing cases, the lead investigator is obvious; it is the investigator running the case, also known as the case agent. This investigator has developed leads, identified the probable cause that evidence exists in the place he wants searched, and obtained a search warrant for the premises. The authority is clear because the lead investigator is there from the beginning.

For emergency crime scenes, however, no lead investigator has been assigned. The first responders have not considered overall jurisdictional issues or which agent in the appropriate agency will respond. They do their jobs as described in the previous chapter, without the supervision of an on-scene investigator. Once the first responders have per-formed health and safety duties, initiated scene security and fully assessed the situation, they then put a call out to their agency so the appropriate specialized investigator responds to the scene. Who this investigator is depends on several factors; the two most important are the investigatory jurisdiction and the type of crime that's been committed.

This main investigator can be called different titles, depending on the specific agency and its governmental level. Often, if the jurisdiction allows for a local police department or sheriff's office, the arriving officer is called the lead detective. If the jurisdiction favors a state or federal agency, the special agent is either the lead investigator or case agent. When writing crime scenes, spend some time researching the appropriate label for your character based on locale, jurisdiction, and type of crime. Keep in mind, though, that no matter the title, this lead investigator has the same responsibilities, regardless of the agency.

> ACCURACY – Governmental levels include local (cities/towns/counties), state, and federal.

The lead investigator often works for a specific unit within their agency. That unit only responds if the crime scene corresponds to its specialties. The different divisions vary greatly agency to agency, but a common breakdown is:

- Violent Crimes Section
  - Homicide/Suspicious Death Unit
  - Missing Persons/Kidnapping Unit
  - Aggravated Assault Unit
  - Aggravated Battery Unit
  - Stalking Unit
  - Kidnapping Unit
  - Arson Unit
- Major Crimes Section
  - Crimes Against Children, Elderly, and Animals Unit
  - Sexual Crimes Unit
  - Domestic Violence Unit
  - Armed Robbery Unit
  - Fraud and Identity Theft Unit
- Drug Task Force Section

Sometimes Homicide, Missing Persons and Sexual Crimes (also known as Special Victims) are made into their own sections.

As I stated above, there is no set standard for how the agency's sections are broken out. So another example of departmental divisions could be:

- Crimes Against Persons Section
  - Homicide/ Suspicious Death Unit
  - Special Victims Unit
  - Missing Persons Unit
  - Assaults Unit

- ○ Robbery Unit
- ○ Domestic Violence Unit
- Crimes Against Property Section
  - ○ Burglary Unit
  - ○ Auto Theft Unit
  - ○ Arsons Unit
  - ○ Financial Crimes Unit
  - ○ Vandalism Unit

Federal agencies have specific crime-type jurisdictional limitations. For example, the Drug Enforcement Administration (DEA) is limited to drug investigations, while the Bureau of Alcohol, Tobacco and Firearms (ATF) can only investigate crimes relating to those topics. Many of these agencies split their sections between Major Crimes and General / Administrative Crimes.

Other federal agencies, such as the FBI or a military investigative agency like the Air Force Office of Special Investigations (AFOSI), have a much broader investigatory directive and therefore break their sections into more specific divisions. Again, if you choose an established agency for your story, make sure to research that agency to get the correct organizational chart.

No matter who the lead investigator is, or whether the crime scene originates from an emergency call or part of an ongoing investigation, from the moment she arrives at the scene, she is in charge. She will get a report from the first responders and assess the situation. It's up to her to determine if the perimeter was set at the appropriate distance, to approve the entrance/exit point location, and to devise the plan for processing the scene. From that point, every person who enters the scene will do so only by her permission. She will take charge of handing out tasks, making the final decisions on what is considered evidence, and dealing with any difficulty encountered during the process.

> **PROCEDURE** – Only one person is in charge at the crime scene. Although the lead investigator might be pressured by bosses or political VIPs, that person has the final say on all matters relating to that scene.

Scene Integrity

The crime scene is only ideal at the time the crime was committed. From that time forward, weather, animal activity, and every person on that scene—from who discovered the crime to the first responders to the investigators themselves—change it. Locard's Exchange Principle applies to all of these people as much as it does the perpetrator. The lead investigator must recognize these alterations of the crime scene and do everything she possibly can to minimize them. Keeping scene integrity is paramount for the pending investigation.

Scene integrity can be kept in many ways. As we

discussed in the last chapter, the primary method is by establishing scene security. The first responders, or in the case of a search warrant, the lead investigator herself, create a perimeter around the area using crime scene tape. When not a civil hindrance, investigators prefer the crime scene area to be as large as possible. In the previous chapter, we discussed the benefits of a large area keeping onlookers at a distance from what's going on in the target scene.

Another reason to make the outside barrier large is so an **inner perimeter** can be established around the target scene. The **target scene** is the actual area that needs to be searched for evidence. Putting up an inner perimeter marks the target scene and is inside the outer barrier. The area between the inner and outer perimeters is a safe zone where on-scene personnel can gather when not actively processing the target scene itself. It provides space for a break area as well as spots to set up or dismantle equipment while protected from the public. The inner perimeter does not need to be created with crime scene tape, but does need to be visible. It can be marked with ribbons on stakes or traffic cones or anything else that will let the responding teams know where they are not to enter.

TERMS – The target scene is the focus of the crime scene, where evidence is expected to be found.

On many scenes, investigators keep the media outside the outer perimeter tape with everyone else. However, on certain high-profile cases, or those receiving pressure from an officer's higher-ups, the lead investigator may choose to give the media a clearly marked area within the outer perimeter (if the scene has an inner perimeter) to occupy. This "media box" will still be placed well away from where the responding officers gather or investigators actively search the target scene for evidence, but still within the protected areas between perimeters. Any media personnel bold enough to step out of the box will be ejected from the scene immediately.

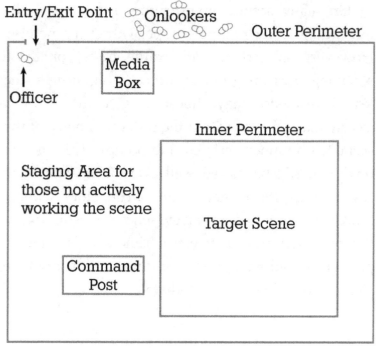

Figure 3: Crime Scene Areas

On more complicated crime scenes, or those in-volving high-profile attention or multiple locations, the lead investigator may prefer to set up a command post in the inner area. The lead investigator uses the command post as the hub that all information passes through. She can display maps, charts, and all investigative information to assist her in making decisions, delegating her assignments, and providing coordination with other related crime scenes. She can always be reached at the command post and can use its location to give briefings to any superior or dignitary requiring updates. The command post becomes an ideal spot to place any significant scene visitors, without worrying they will inadvertently contaminate the scene. It also provides an area where specialists can lay out and account for their equipment. Simpler scenes do not require a command post and the lead investigator can herself participate in the actual processing of the scene.

Crime Scene Pathway

An additional method of preserving scene integrity is to control where everyone goes within the target scene itself. Once officers have established the crime scene perimeter, the lead investigator needs to make an assessment of the target scene. She will determine the pathway that will become the only route everyone will take onto and off of the scene until the entire scene has been fully processed. She takes the crime scene sketcher with her through the scene (addressed more fully in the next chapter) so that he can create a workable map for those not on the scene and can record anything the lead investigator deems important during her walk-through.

The perimeter entry/exit point will serve as the beginning of the path, as it is already established and has a log of everyone entering and leaving. Any evidence on or significantly near this pathway will be collected immediately, because its proximity renders it **perishable** (or **transient**) **evidence**.

Perishable evidence has the potential to change

over time. Anything that naturally degrades is perishable, such as a piece of fruit that for whatever reason may contain evidentiary value (if it has a bite mark in it, for example). However, investigators also consider items that would not necessarily change on their own as perishable if they are found on the crime scene pathway, regardless of their susceptibility to decomposition or disintegration.

As mentioned above, the pathway is where all of the foot traffic into, through, and out of the scene is directed. Evidence with the potential to be stepped on or kicked is considered perishable because such actions change the evidence from its original location. All perishable evidence is collected at the time the pathway is established to preserve its utility and context.

Crime Scene Equipment

Many crime scene investigators carry a crime scene kit with them wherever they go. A **crime scene kit** is a portable case containing the equipment needed at a crime scene. Because the reason investigators establish and search crime scenes is to identify and collect evidence, the vast majority of crime scene equipment can be placed into three categories:

- Personal protective equipment protects the investigators from the evidence and vice versa.
- Evidence markers allow the investigators to

disclose the location of each piece of evidence so they can come back to collect it later.

- Evidence collection equipment consist of containers and materials that aid investigators in taking each piece of evidence.

Various specialized equipment specific to certain situations can also supplement a basic crime scene kit. Specialized equipment is anything investigators use for the collection of very specific evidence. For example, officers use fingerprint powders and brushes to lift fingerprints. Certain chemical compounds detect blood. Swabbing kits collect potential gunshot residue. Each agency determines what specialized equipment to include in their own crime scene kits and what has to be brought to the scene separately, depending on their primary mission and budget.

Personal Protective Equipment (PPE) is any of a variety of outer layer disposable clothing. It consists of latex gloves, shoe booties, sleeves, goggles, aprons, masks, and full bio-hazard "bunny" suits. There are several reasons that PPE is important at a crime scene, the foremost being, as the name suggests, for an investigator's personal protection. Many crime scenes can introduce potential hazards to an investigator, especially those involving blood. PPE provides a barrier to keep any sort of pathogen from infecting the officer.

CRIME SCENES (FORENSICS FOR FICTION SERIES)

Conversely, PPE also protects the scene from the investigator. Keep Locard's Exchange Principle in mind. Every time another investigator enters the crime scene, that person is at some level contaminating it. PPE can prevent the investigator from leaving his own marks on the scene. For example, latex gloves can prevent wasted hours of collecting the investigator's own fingerprints by preventing them from being left behind in the first place. PPE can also be vital in protecting additional crime scenes from cross-contamination, which is a concept we'll discuss later.

Evidence markers are just that, items placed to indicate evidence locations so they can be easily found later. During a search, investigators do not pause to collect the evidence as it's found, which procedurally becomes inefficient. They continue the search until the entire area is covered, marking each piece of evidence so they can readily come back to it.

If everything was done at once, the searches would be too chaotic, as each piece of evidence has to be photographed numerous times and annotated on the sketch with triangulated measurements. The photographer and sketcher would be running all over the scene, and while they were conducting the proper annotations in one section, the searches of the other sections would be held up waiting on them.

Using evidence markers makes the search process much more efficient. Once police have completely

CHAPTER 3: CRIME SCENE PROCESSING

searched an area, the photographer and sketcher can cover the entire section at once, which frees those officers to search the next section, or perform other tasks requested by the lead investigator. After each section has been photographed and sketched, the searchers can return when convenient and collect all of the marked evidence. The evidence markers both show the investigators where the evidence is and also help protect against overlooking any evidence.

Evidence markers can be just about anything, as long as they are easily visible and numbered. Most commonly, they are small plastic fluorescent-yellow A-frames with big black numbers. Sometimes the colors are neon-green or orange, but most common is yellow. Evidence markers can also come as small, brightly colored, and numbered cones. For evidence on vertical surfaces, such as a wall, tape in the form of arrows is also used. Most tapes require the investigator to annotate the number by hand.

Figure 4: Evidence A-Frame Markers

Figure 5: Evidence Marker Arrow Tape

The most important factor for these markers is they must be unique in their numbering. In court, if the prosecution or defense wants to look at a picture of the evidence marked by marker "12," a second "12" cannot exist at the scene. Often, investigators find more evidence than they have markers available. Searchers can address this problem in many ways.

First, if the lead investigator has broken the entire scene down into sections, she gives each section an identification, such as "A," "B," and so forth. The searchers then label each marker in that section with that identification. For example, the first evidence marker used in section A would be marked "A1." That way the searchers can reuse evidence marker "1" in section B, as long as they relabel it as "B1."

Another method is to use all of the markers, collect that evidence, and then reuse the markers by adjusting their labeling. So if there are 50 markers, the investigators would mark and then collect evidence 1–50, mark and then collect evidence 1a–50a, and then evidence 1b–50b, and so on. An alternative way of relabeling is to add a "1" to each marker, changing markers 1–50 to 101–150, and then, if needed, changing that to 201–250, and so on.

In some situations, one evidence marker can be used for several pieces of evidence. This is a trickier method, and great care must be taken to identify everything the evidence marker is representing. For example, on a drive-by shooting scene, a searcher can use one marker to identify six shell casings that are relatively close together on the ground. If the evidence marker was "3" when the casings are collected, each casing needs to be carefully annotated as evidence numbers "3-1" through "3-6," or "3-a" through "3-f" or something similar. And "3-a" must be unique and differentiated from "3A" if "3A" is used elsewhere in the scene. You can see how careful the investigators need to be with this method, and why it may not always be advisable. Carelessness when labeling evidence markers introduces confusion and has undermined too many cases even before they came to trial.

> **PROCEDURE** – Every evidence marker used to locate evidence must be uniquely labeled from every other marker on the scene.

The lead investigator can employ whatever labeling method she chooses, as long as it differentiates carefully between each piece of evidence.

When discussing evidence numbering, I want to make a clear distinction. Everything stated above relates to the different methods of labeling evidence markers, which show where the evidence is *physically located* so it can be collected later. When investigators actually *collect* each piece, however, it is annotated in the evidence log *sequentially*, from number "1" up through however many pieces of evidence are seized. The marker's number does not necessarily mirror the evidence log number. For example, evidence markers

1–50 may line up perfectly with evidence log entries 1–50; however, if the next piece of evidence is for evidence marker location "1a," that would still be evidence log number "51." Each evidence log entry will annotate which evidence marker location number was assigned to it so the crime scene pictures correlate correctly, but the evidence log itself will be a cohesive, sequential list.

Evidence collection equipment includes anything that helps collect and store evidence. It consists of paper bags, sealable plastic bags, glass jars, unused paint cans, swabs, disposable tweezers, evidence tape, evidence tags, an evidence log, and chain of custody forms.

Evidence labels are typically printed on the paper and plastic bags themselves, but everything else requires an adhesive label that can be affixed after investigators collect the evidence.

As mentioned above, many kinds of evidence require their own methods of detection and collection. The types of evidence and the individual techniques used to collect each kind are too numerous to include in a book of this length. So, I'm going to focus on how to find the evidence and leave the specific collection techniques for their own dedicated book.

Search Patterns

Once the lead investigator has surveyed the scene and taken care of all of the set-up, she now needs to decide the best method of processing the scene.

- Does she want to divide the target area into sections and assign a different searcher to each?
- Does she want each section searched by an individual or a team?
- Is the scene massive enough that calling in for volunteer searchers is the best option?
- Do factors such as weather make one area a higher priority than another?

She needs to consider all of these variables and then assign duties. She can choose from several search patterns, depending on which she thinks is the best fit for the area she's dealing with.

A line search is typically done outdoors, especially when covering a massive amount of ground. Volunteers are needed to help with this search pattern. All of the searchers stand in a straight line to the left and right of their neighboring searchers and are equidistant from each other. As a group, everyone advances together in a straight line, searching the area in their vicinity. If someone thinks they found something, the entire line stops. Having everyone act in unison allows the investigators to keep control of the large number people. This search technique is most typically used in a missing child case because it can rapidly cover a large area.

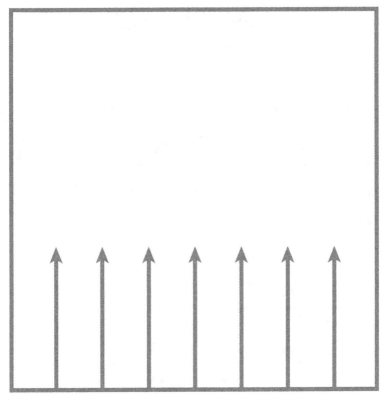

Figure 6: Line Search Pattern

A <u>spiral search</u> is another pattern typically done outside, especially if the outer border of the search area is known, such as in a field. In this pattern, the searchers first cover the farthest border circle surrounding the search area. Once they have searched that circle, the team moves inward and searches the next smaller circular area. Each circle moves inward, getting smaller and working toward the main focus area of the search, until they have covered the entire area.

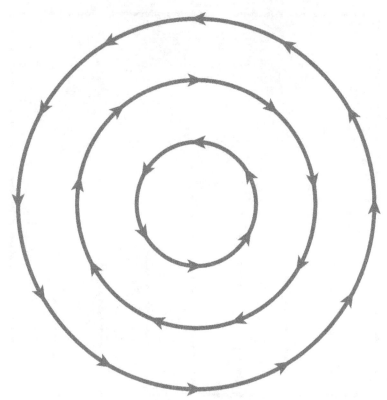

Figure 7: Spiral Search Pattern

A <u>lane search</u> is good indoors or out, for big areas or small. Searchers can use it over an entire area or in smaller, individual sections. This pattern is typically used when a limited number of searchers are available, because it's so adaptable. Basically, the searchers go up and down the search area, searching their immediate vicinity as they go. They continue searching in this up-then-down pattern until the entire area is covered.

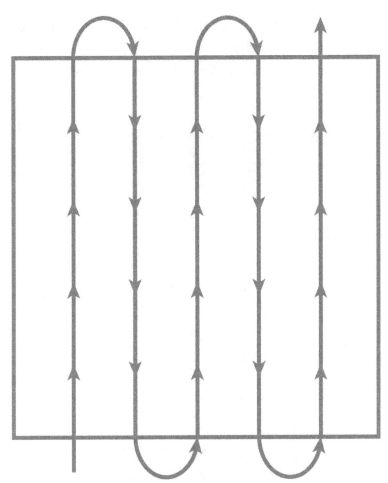

Figure 8: Lane Search Pattern

The <u>grid search</u> is simply a more thorough lane search, and can be done in all of the same areas. This method follows the lane pattern but then redoes the entire area from the other direction to cover the area twice. So, after searchers follow the lane search pattern by going up and down until the entire area is covered, they then search the same area again perpendicularly by going left and right. If time allows, the grid pattern is simply a more exhaustive search, ensuring no evidence has been missed.

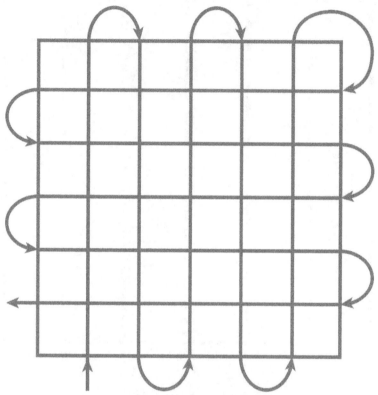

Figure 9: Grid Search Pattern

A <u>zone search</u> is ideal indoors and involves dividing the overall search area into very small sections that can be covered by a searcher without any additional pattern. In a house, each room would be a different zone. The key to its success is that the search area must be small enough that one searcher can manageably process it without missing any evidence.

A larger area, such as the inside of a warehouse or the outdoors, can be divided into zones as well, as long as each zone is small and well-defined. Another term for this pattern is a quadrant search, because it divides the entire area into four equal quadrants. Investigators can further divide each quadrant into subquadrants until the divisions are small enough to be manageable for the searcher(s).

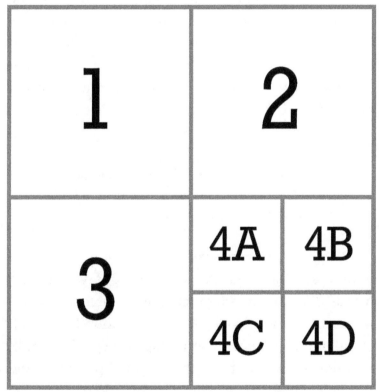

Figure 10: Zone or Quadrant Search Pattern

Searching Pitfalls

When everything has been set for the search to finally begin, there is what may seem a self-evident dictum for crime scenes that is unfortunately often unheeded: *Let the scene tell the tale.*

If investigators reach a conclusion about what happened even before arriving at the scene, they will become tunnel-visioned and, as strange as it sounds, only find the evidence that supports that specific, preordained theory. They may explain away or altogether overlook any other evidence. That's why even if a body is hanging by the neck in an apartment, officers must process that scene as if the crime is a homicide until the evidence proves it's suicide. Many murderers stage their crimes to appear to be suicides.

> **PITFALL –** Tunnel vision is a real problem when processing a crime scene. Investigators need to let the scene tell the story, and never force it to tell theirs.

Another common error during searches is immediately focusing on the obvious, glitzy evidence. Minus life-saving attempts, going directly to and processing the proximate area around a body straightaway is *always* the wrong strategy. Hopefully you noticed in all of the above search patterns, none of them began the search in the middle of the scene. They all began at the outer edge and worked their way in.

A body, for example, may be the most spectacular

part of a crime scene, but the body does not contain the evidence of how the murderer got in or exited, or the footprints left behind, or the plethora of other evidence needed to piece this scene together. The area around the body will still be there when the investigators reach it, but focusing on it too early can result in incorrect assumptions and a significant amount of evidence being missed.

> PITFALL – Processing a scene is a methodical, often slow process. Rushing to the exciting evidence is never an appropriate strategy.

Death Scenes

I must address one important distinction with regard to corpses.

When a crime scene includes a deceased person, typically referred to as a **death scene**, the lead investigator has no authority over the collection or handling of the body. Because investigators are not medical doctors, they do not have the training, expertise, or authority to declare a person dead. If they cannot make this determination, they cannot, and should not, be able to move or otherwise affect the remains in any capacity, because if there is even the slightest chance the person is still alive, they risk causing greater harm. All remains are the responsibility of the appropriate county coroner or medical examiner (ME) .

> **TERMS – A death scene is simply a crime scene that has a dead body on it.**

The lead investigator may continue with her scene processing while she's waiting for the coroner/ME, but she cannot do any search of the body. Once the coroner/ME arrives and determines the body is dead, he will annotate a time of death, which is the time of death pronouncement, not the exact time the person ceased living. The medical crew will then collect the remains and transport them to the coroner's/medical examiner's office. Any search of the body will typically be done in the presence of a law enforcement representative attending the autopsy, which may be a day or so later.

> **PROCEDURE – A dead body is off-limits to the lead investigator. Any processing or moving of the remains is done by the responding coroner or medical examiner.**

Because the body is removed from the crime scene, investigators used to draw a chalk outline around the body before it was transported. This way investigators could still visualize the person's positioning after removal. These days chalk outlines are no longer used, as crime scene sketches and photography provide the necessary details and measurements for crime reconstruction. A body's location in the room has become much more significant than its positioning. The body of a face-down person with his arm above his head, for example, does not necessarily prove he was reaching for something. The position of the arm may simply be where it ended up when the person fell at that location. As forensic techniques have expanded our understanding of crime scenes, investigators have moved beyond more primitive "eyeball" evidence which relies on impressions and surmises in favor of science and hard data.

> ACCURACY – Although many writers still use chalk outlines in their books for effect (like the cover of this one!), they are really a relic of an earlier time in crime scene processing.

Although we've covered what happens during the set-up and searching of a crime scene, crime scene sketchers and photographers are recording the scene simultaneously. Their duties, from arrival to completion, become essential for scene reconstruction.

Case Study #1: JonBenét Ramsey – Chaotic Scenes Beget Chaotic Cases

The JonBenét Ramsey investigation remains one of the most compelling unsolved murders in American history. There are two primary theories for this case: JonBenét died at the hands of a Ramsey family member (an insider) or an intruder. As the case became more sensationalized, the more viewers, reporters, and even the investigative agencies became entrenched in either one camp or the other. This investigation became a case of misdirection, conclusion out of speculation, ego, and politics. But, putting all of the extraneous aside, if you boil this case down to its barest details, it cannot be solved for one reason: investigators did not process the crime scene appropriately.

Everything else is just hysterical byproduct.

JonBenét was six years old at the time of her death. She was the daughter of John and Patsy Ramsey and three years younger than her brother, Burke. John Ramsey owned a software company and provided an affluent life for his family. They lived in a fifteen-room mansion in Boulder, Colorado, owned a plane and a boat, and were influential in city politics.

For both theories in this case, the layout of the house became pivotal. It was a three-story residence with a basement. The primary stairs were at the front of the house, located next to the basement stairs. There was a spiral staircase at the rear of the house that also connected the main and second floors, and another staircase beside it that connect the second and third (top) floors. John and Patsy used the entire top floor for their bedroom and dressing areas. JonBenét's and Burke's bedrooms were on the second floor, but on opposite sides of the house, separated by a playroom and a guest bedroom.

For the intruder theory, the layout and locations of the family can lean toward explaining why a scream may not necessarily have been heard. For the insider theory, the layout raises questions about the Ramseys' movements that morning, which don't always seem the most logical.

According to the Ramseys in different interviews, nothing out of the ordinary happened on Christmas Day, 1996: the kids were up early, the family exchanged presents, neighborhood kids came by to play, and John finalized plans to take the family on a trip the following day to visit his adult children from a previous marriage. They spent Christmas evening at the house of their good friends, Fleet and Priscilla White. They ate with the Whites, and returned home at approximately nine o'clock that evening.

John claimed JonBenét fell asleep in the car on the way home, so he immediately carried her to bed. Burke wanted to put together one of his Christmas toys, and Patsy worked on finishing getting ready for their trip. John said he helped Burke with the toy, put him to bed and then went to bed himself.

According to their interviews, John and Patsy got up between five and six AM the following morning, December 26, 1996, because they were going to have to leave early for their trip. Patsy claimed she put on the same clothes she wore the day before and eventually went down the back-of-the-house spiral staircase on her way to the kitchen to make coffee. Those subscribing to the theory that a family member committed the murder theorize that Patsy was in the same clothes because she was up all night and never took them off.

Patsy stated as she was descending the stairs that morning, she noticed a three-page note on one of the steps. She picked it up and realized it was a ransom note.

There are a few strange behaviors here.

First is the fact that the ransom note was left on the back staircase. The entire purpose of a ransom note is to leave a message. An intruder needs for the family to receive the message, not for it to be over-looked. So why would a kidnapper leave the note on the back staircase? Historically, a note is left on a prominent surface, such as the dining table, at the entrance to the house, or on the kitchen counter. Kidnappers typically leave it at a place where it cannot be missed.

Moreover, the back stairs do not lead to the kitch-en; they lead to a corner of two hallways and the mud room, off of the garage. How did the alleged intruder anticipate the Ramsey family members' actions? How would he know Patsy or someone else would use those stairs instead of the main stairway? That was a big risk, because, had the three Ramseys used the front stairs, the more convenient choice for their respective bedrooms, the note could have been missed.

The third strange-yet-lucky assumption on the part of an alleged intruder involved his timing. The note said the ransom call would come between eight and ten o'clock, but was not completely clear whether it would be that morning or the next day. If the kidnapper intended to call that morning, how did he know the Ramseys would even be up that early the day after Christmas? It seems oddly convenient that Patsy was able to find the almost out-of-the-way note with enough time to get police and friends mobilized before the call was to come in.

Upon finding the note, Patsy claimed she started screaming, ran back up the stairs and opened Jon-Benét's bedroom door to find her missing. She then ran to Burke's room, where he reportedly was still sleeping, left him there, and screamed for John. When John read the note, he told Patsy to call the police.

At 5:52 AM a hysterical Patsy called 911. Investigators noted three items of interest in that call, all of which made the 911 operator, Kimberly Archuleta, feel something was very wrong with Patsy's story.

First, Archuleta said she was surprised at the brevity of the call. In her experience, parents want to stay on the phone until the police arrive, holding on to a lifeline and as a way to find out what to do. They also continually want updates on where the police are. Patsy didn't do that. She reported the kidnapping, pleaded for help, and then ended the call.

Second, the audio tape shows the call did not disconnect when Patsy thought she hung up the phone. Archuleta said as soon as Patsy was off the phone, her hysteria evaporated, and her tone of voice exhibited a completely different affect.

Third, Archuleta said she heard three distinct voices from the Ramsey house. This is significant because it counters the Ramseys' claim that Burke never got out of bed. Audio enhancement of the tape does reveal talking after Patsy left the conversation with Archuleta. The Boulder Police and those subscribing to the theory that the murderer was one of the Ramseys claim they can make out what was said and who said it. Those with the intruder theory claim the enhancement only airs misinterpreted background noise.

At 5:54 AM, Patsy disconnected the call and began calling friends. Law enforcement found this behavior strange as well. Unless there is someone a victim has grown to rely on solely for emotional support, like a loved one or extremely close friend, typically a family waits for the police to arrive before reaching out to friends. Remember, the police were already on their way, and arrived at 5:59 AM. Hysterical or not, Patsy had no reason to start calling all of her friends at that point in time. Further, the note specifically said the Ramsey household was being watched, and if they told anyone (even a "stray dog"), JonBenét would be killed. Having a group of friends come to the house seemed extremely risky, if not reckless behavior for parents of a missing child in these circumstances.

The next few hours were critical for this investigation, and reveal the reason I'm focusing on this particular case in this book. What law enforcement allowed to happen, as well as what they did not do, set this entire case up for failure.

They did not secure that crime scene.

There was no scene security and absolutely no scene integrity. A tainted scene cannot provide anything but tainted evidence.

The timeline went essentially as follows:

- Between 6:00 AM and 7:00 AM
  - Multiple friends arrived and were allowed by law enforcement to enter the house. When there were too many to all console Patsy at the same time, the rest began to loiter. Some tried to keep busy and started cleaning, especially in the kitchen. Others wandered the house.
  - Detectives arrived and started preparing in case the ransom call came in between 8:00 AM and 10:00 AM.
  - Fleet White took Burke to his house and then returned.
  - John called his banker to try and get the ransom money in the denominations specified.
- 8:00 AM
  - Detectives called the FBI, which has jurisdiction in kidnapping cases.
  - Some crime scene photos were taken outside and within the home, but a thorough search was not conducted.
  - No ransom call came in during the specified timeframe (or any time after).
- 11:00 AM
  - FBI Agent Ron Walker arrived from Denver, but went to the Boulder Police

Department instead of the Ramseys' home to review the ransom note and set up a command post.

- 11:45 AM
  - All but two of the detectives left the home to go meet with Special Agent Walker at Boulder PD. Detective Linda Arndt was one of the two left behind with a houseful of people.
- 1:00 PM
  - Detective Arndt gave a status report and said she had not been able to keep up with John Ramsey's whereabouts for over an hour.
  - Agent Walker directed Arndt to give John a task to keep him both busy and trackable.
  - Arndt instructed John to search the house top to bottom and look for anything out of the ordinary.
  - John immediately grabbed Fleet White and headed to the basement, without Arndt.
- 1:05 PM
  - John found JonBenét's body in the back room of the basement, wrapped in a blanket. She had duct tape on her mouth, her hands were bound and she had a strangling garrote so tight it was buried in her neck.

- ○ A distraught John removed the duct tape, untied one hand and then carried the body upstairs. He laid the body down in the hallway.
- 1:10 PM
  - ○ Detective Arndt moved the body from the hallway to the living room.
  - ○ John covered the body with a sheet.
- 1:20 PM
  - ○ The detectives from the police station returned to the scene along with Special Agent Walker.
  - ○ The Boulder Police Department regained jurisdiction in the investigation from the FBI because the case had gone from a kidnapping to a murder.

The Boulder County Coroner conducted the autopsy on December 27, 1996. The report was submitted months later and found the cause of death to be asphyxia by strangulation associated with craniocerebral (front skull and brain) trauma. The assailant hit JonBenét on the head with enough force to break her skull, but not tear her scalp. Her head bled internally and her brain swelled, meaning she was still alive after the blow. The garrote strangled her so tightly that it shaved an area of skin off of her neck as it moved its way up. Marks on her neck indicated she may have tried to claw at the ligature, also implying she was alive when it was applied. There was a small amount of undigested food in her stomach consistent with pineapple. Because we know she ate dinner at the Whites', yet only pineapple was found during the autopsy, the pineapple had to have been ingested after the body had time to digest the dinner, but prior to death. A dead body cannot swallow, so the pineapple could not have been forced into her digestive system after death.

The early mistakes investigators made in this seven-hour period damaged the investigation irrevocably. Evidence from a contaminated scene has to be excessively strong and decidedly clear to overcome the question marks put over it. No evidence in this case could rise to that standard. All that's left are speculative theories, which, as the investigation progressed, erroneously evolved into all-or-nothing opposing truths.

As background, I need to establish the critical environment under which this investigation existed. At that time, the United States was still recovering from the media frenzy that was the O.J. Simpson trial. That not-guilty verdict occurred just over a year prior, and no law enforcement agency or prosecutor's office wanted to work under that same scrutiny again. But the 24-hour news reporters couldn't wait for their next Crime of the Century.

The pressure of working under that kind of scrutiny is immense. The public records and analyzes every move. They spread every theory as if it is fact. Every layperson has a critical opinion on what should be done and how. Elected officials such as the mayor and district attorney now have to worry about keeping the public happy on top of their other duties. Law enforcement has to try to use the media as a tool while simultaneously keeping it at bay. It's a precarious situation at best.

The Boulder PD established no crime scene prior to JonBenét's body being found. Detectives did go around and take crime scene photos in and around the house, but they were not exhaustive, or else JonBenét would have been found much earlier. Although the detectives needed to wait for the FBI and they had every indication that this was a kidnapping, a perimeter should have been established, and no one should have been allowed into that house. Since it was initially believed to be a kidnapping, the existence of the note meant a perpetrator had been inside the house, which meant evidence of him was there as well. No valid reason exists for the scene to not have been secured. Even if friends were permitted to enter the scene, for whatever reason, they should have been strictly corralled into one room and not allowed to walk about.

Instead, the friends had access to the entire house, potentially destroying evidence of the intruder, or covering it with their own. Not only that, police permitted restless visitors to *clean* the house before establishing a perimeter. Every dish they washed, floor they swept, or counter they wiped down threw any evidence there out with the trash.

Investigators should have kept John and Patsy in a single room until they were removed individually for interviews. Officers on the scene should never have allowed John to disappear for over an hour, and certainly should never have instructed him to search his own house. Law enforcement should have begun the search the moment they arrived.

Because they allowed John to find JonBenét's body, he was also able to remove the duct tape and tamper with the ligature on JonBenét's hands. If the assailant had been an intruder, any of the outsider's evidence could have been covered, destroyed, or removed by these actions.

John then brought JonBenét upstairs and laid her down in the hallway, right where so many people had recently walked and loitered. There is no telling what sort of visitors' evidence accumulated on the body because of this action, such as touch DNA, for example.

Detective Arndt then picked the body back up and put it in the living room, where John put a sheet on JonBenét's body, risking even greater evidence contamination. According to Locard's Exchange

Principle, that sheet took evidence off of the body and put its own trace elements on it.

The open scene had no integrity, meaning any evidence found could have a legitimate reason for being there because of all the people present, if any evidence was left to find at all. No evidence found at this scene could hold any certainty of origin or purpose. Everything from this point on was fiasco.

Earlier in this book, I warned against entering a crime scene with a specific theory already in mind. In those cases, the evidence found and evaluated will always be molded to fit that theory. I argue that dangerous agenda occurred twice in this case, and is why both prevailing theories here are so passionately defended.

In order for any layperson to make up his own mind about this investigation, he must consider all of the evidence on all of the topics raised in this case and evaluate the pros and the cons that evidence presents to both of the primary theories.

The topics within the JonBenét investigation that a *thorough* case study must analyze include the ransom note itself, where it was written, how it was written, what it said, where it was left, the open broken window in the basement, the suitcase under that window, the pineapple on the counter, the garrote, the wounds assumed to be from a stun gun, the DNA found in the panties, and the touch DNA found on the leggings many years later. Also, reviewers must consider the theories of sexual abuse, bedwetting, the family's behavior throughout the investigation, and the stubborn infighting between the Boulder PD and the Boulder District Attorney's Office in regards to this investigation.

All of these considerations, however, go beyond the scope of this book, and none of them affect the conclusion made here: the flawed crime scene eliminated the chance for this case to be solved. If you're interested in more detailed discussion, I do provide a complete analysis of all aspects of this case, which you can read at www.geoffsymon.com/jonbenet.

Had investigators processed and secured the initial scene immediately and appropriately, I believe the case would never have been allowed to descend into the chaos it did. That is why the concepts in this book are so important. Crime scene security, crime scene control, and crime scene integrity are vital to the successful resolution of every case.

Chapter 4: Crime Scene Documentation

Crime scene reconstruction is vital to an investigation. Once a crime scene has been processed for evidence and released, the value of that physical scene drops dramatically. Should the investigator need to come back at a later date, she can no longer claim anything in the scene is as it was during the crime. Moreover, any investigation presents a significant disruption to those who live or work at that scene. Investigators need to be able to re-create the scene without the necessity of physically going to it. They do this by completely documenting the scene while they are processing it.

Sketches

We live in a digital age, but hand-drawn crime scene sketches remain an essential tool when processing the site. They provide an immediate on-scene representation of the area while allowing for notes and comparisons. They are useful in providing a bird's-eye view of the entire area and memorializing an item's location and proximity to other items. As we'll discuss below, determining distances via photographs is extremely difficult. A sketch enables accurate reconstruction of the scene and specific placement of the furniture, evidence, and other items present with reliable measurements.

> **PROCEDURE – The sketch artist's primary job is to draw a representation of the scene on paper and to provide significant measurements so that the scene can be recreated perfectly at a different time, to include placing evidence back in its exact position.**

I've already mentioned the sketcher accompanies the lead investigator during the initial scene walkthrough. During this time, the sketcher creates a rough representation of the scene (with landmarks such as a tree stump or driveway if outside, or room sizes and configurations if inside). The sketcher is present to annotate anything in the sketch that the lead investigator deems important. The lead investigator then uses the sketch to determine the appropriate search patterns, how to divvy up the scene into sections, and which areas take higher priority. After searchers have covered each area and marked all evidence locations, the sketcher needs to add these pieces of evidence to the sketch.

PROCEDURE: A sketch, no matter how amateur, is vital to a crime scene because of the accuracy it provides. Without a sketch, any reconstruction can at best be an approximation, which does not carry any deductive significance.

Some law enforcement agencies may have strict rules when it comes to crime scene sketching, but the vast majority do not. Some agencies have designated sketchers who respond to crime scenes, but most often sketching is a duty assigned while on site.

The sketcher does not need to be an artist, and the most amateur of sketches are still acceptable. Rarely are the sketches to scale, and the most simplistic shapes are drawn to represent furniture, vehicles, and other items present. Any shorthand or symbols used on the sketch are up to the sketcher, as long as they can be interpreted accurately at a later date. Therefore, if a sketcher is annotating a footprint, he can draw a tiny footprint, or if he is not comfortable doing that, he can draw a dot, an "x," an "FP," or any other representation that he will know means it's a footprint. If he doesn't draw the actual print, though, he must take care to annotate its orientation—the direction it was pointing within the scene. Again, how he does this is up to him, as long as he can accurately recreate what was found in the scene.

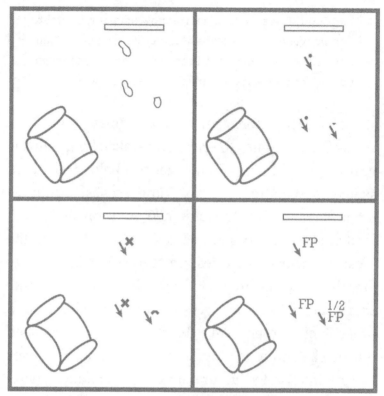

Figure 11: Different Valid Footprint Representations in a Rough Crime Scene Sketch

Although the annotation techniques may vary greatly, each sketch must contain the following:

- Any immovable environmental objects for measurements (trees, roads, mailboxes, windows, doors, support beams, etc.).
- Significant environmental objects within the scene and their orientation for reference (tables, chairs, clothes hampers, garbage bins, vehicles, etc.).

- All evidence.
- Accurate distance measurements for everything. We'll discuss a technique called triangulation below.
- A compass indicating north.

In order for the scene to be recreated at a later date, accuracy is key when creating the crime scene sketch. Investigators need to know that the footprint was found at a specific spot in the room, and not just in the room in general. The term for adding measurements to a sketch is **mapping**. Random or insufficient mapping, however, does not aid the investigator. Just a few measurements that show the length and width of the room, for example, may be useful information, but do not provide the detailed accuracy that pinpoints the location of the evidence in that room.

For appropriate precision, sketch artists primarily use a mapping technique called **triangulation** on the sketch. This method takes two measurements originating from known points to the item of significance, such as a piece of evidence. A known point is something that will not change over time. The corner of a doorframe will be in the same spot if you come back in five minutes or a year. Likewise, a tree will not move, nor will a support column in a room. However, the edge of a table will not work as a known point because a table *can* be moved. There is no way to tell where exactly in the room a movable object was, so the measurement to the evidence does not accurately place that evidence within the scene. For the same reason, a car, or any other movable object, cannot be used in triangulation.

> TERMS – Triangulation is a technique used in crime scene sketching that accurately annotates an item's location by using two measurements to the item originating from fixed known points.

The accuracy of triangulation comes from using *two* measurements for each piece of evidence. One measurement does not suffice. If a piece of evidence is measured at two feet from a column, you cannot place the evidence in the room accurately because there are an infinite number of placements that are two feet away from that column. Put together, all of those placements form a two-foot ring around the column. Adding a second measurement solves this problem by creating a specific point where both measurements meet. If the second measurement shows the evidence is five feet from the corner of the room, only one spot in the entire room exists that is both two feet from the column and five feet from the corner, and that's the exact spot where the evidence was found.

As mentioned above, the sketch artist does not have to be a skilled illustrator. As a matter of fact, the below sketch is perfectly valid (and is the quality you see most often at scenes):

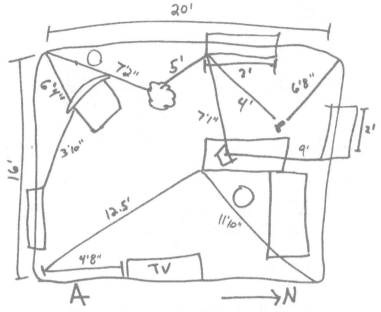

Figure 12: On-scene Rough Crime Scene Sketch

The reason this extremely rough sketch is acceptable is, although it doesn't look very pretty, you can still return to that scene and recreate it with accuracy because of the measurements. Also, once the sketch artist gets back to the station, he can take the time to pull out some graph paper and make a much nicer rendition:

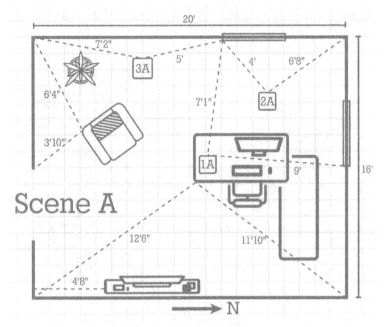

Figure 13: Post-scene To Scale Final Crime Scene Sketch

This is referred to as the final sketch, and is what is presented at trial. The original rough sketch becomes part of the agent's notes. The final sketch is drawn to scale and rendered as accurately as possible. Some final sketches are done by computer programs to provide the clearest representation of the scene.

Sometimes for indoor scenes, evidence can be found on the walls. In these cases, some sketches may be made from the observer's head-on point of view, as opposed to the typical overhead perspective. In these cases, the completed full scene sketch is presented with the usual bird's-eye view of the floor, then each head-on wall sketch is added, flattened out on each side. This is called an Exploded View Sketch.

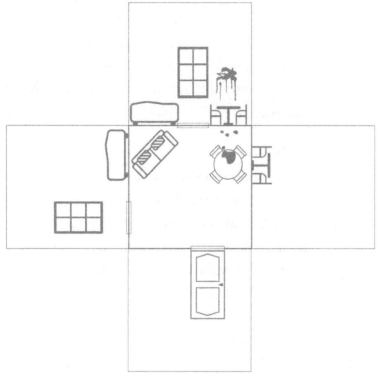

Figure 14: Exploded View Sketch Showing Blood Spatter in a Room

I can't stress enough the importance of a crime scene sketch when reconstructing the crime scene. What are some ways you as an author can use a crime scene sketch to introduce conflict and drama?

- No crime scene sketch, which leaves scene reconstruction relying solely on the scene photographs, which, as we'll see in the next section, can be inaccurate.
- Missing or imprecise measurements. For

example, if the length of the room is recorded incorrectly, the defense can then question every other measurement on the sketch.

- Evidence shown in photographs that does not appear on the sketch (or vice versa).
- A final sketch that does not perfectly match the rough sketch.

Photographs

Crime scene photography is essential to every investigation. Photos provide an accurate account of how things looked at the scene in a way that neither the sketches nor written reports can. They allow the legal system to view the scene without having to be at the physical location during trial. They also permit forensic experts to conduct specific reviews, such as blood spatter analysis and fingerprint comparisons, at a later date. Photos cannot replace crime scene sketches, however, because a two-dimensional photograph can distort the spatial relationships used to determine the distance between two objects. Two photographers standing at the same spot, taking a picture of the same two objects, can show a different measurement between the two objects just by holding the cameras at the slightest angle difference. Depth of field, which can change with the lens and aperture settings, can also distort perceived distances.

Normally, each crime scene has a law enforcement officer who is assigned the duty of taking photographs, but there are times, mostly because of limited personnel, that the photos are taken by the lead investigator. Although an experienced crime scene photographer can take many of the standard pictures without supervision, all photographs are ultimately directed by the lead investigator.

Before we get into specialized crime scene photography techniques, I want to give an overview of photography basics for those who might find that helpful.

> ALERT – The following sections become more technical than most writers need for their stories. It covers photography history, concepts, and terms law enforcement photographers need to be familiar with. Those needing just the essential procedures of crime scene photography can skip the next few sections to the one titled "Photographing the Scene."

While much of the next two sections may seem like minutia, the complexities of photography create limitless opportunities for an author to alter, distort, and derail an investigation either through mistakes, misrepresentation, or manipulation by interested parties. Photographs often provide the bulk of evidence from a scene, and knowing how they are produced gives you (and your characters) a chance to rewrite history and conceal a crime.

Film vs. Digital

The digital revolution has changed photography. These days we all carry cameras as part of the computers/phones in our pockets. It should seem an obvious conclusion that law enforcement would strive to be on the forward edge of such technological advances. Unfortunately, that's not always true. Budgets rarely allow for the quick adoption of the newest technologies and techniques. Perhaps less obviously, law enforcement also needs to ensure that any procedural change fits within the rules of evidence and is protected from scrutiny in court.

Digital photography brings with it many advantages over film:

- It's cost effective. After the initial equipment purchase, there are no recurring charges for film or its development.
- It's timely. There is no wait for film development. A picture can be evaluated immediately after it's taken, and the shot can be retaken if it did not turn out.
- It has more capacity. Film limits the photographer to the number of pictures on a roll and how many rolls are available. Normally, that would be a couple hundred photos. With digital, a single memory card can hold thousands of shots.
- It's more reliable. Although there is the danger

of erasing data, officers no longer have to worry about film's shelf life, or a picture fading over time.

For many years, law enforcement agencies resisted going digital for one specific reason: film photographs are much more difficult to manipulate. With digital photography, there are now apps for almost any manipulation a layman photographer wants to make. Want to change how something looks? A few clicks can add a mask, change a color, or eliminate something in the image altogether. The ease of manipulation raised the question of the validity of digital crime scene photographs at the court level.

Ultimately, digital photography became the norm. Court rulings and precedence established that crime scene photos are considered just like any other piece of evidence admitted at trial. The presenting officer can be challenged if an issue is suspected, at which point it's up to the jury or presiding judge to decide how valuable his evidence is. Therefore, as with any other evidence, the officer is scrutinized to determine the photos' validity.

To safeguard against this scrutiny, most law enforcement agencies immediately create a CD of all the photos, which goes into the evidence room. Everything else to do with the photos can be done with copies on the investigator's computer. The CD, which has a chain of custody proving it was held as evidence since the date the photos were taken, can be used to show any photo presented at court is unchanged.

Camera Settings

A camera is similar to a human eye in that a captured image depends on two main factors, light and focus. All cameras follow the same basic mechanisms: light enters a lens and is recorded on a sensor (what used to be film). A shutter determines when and for how long light can enter the camera. Changing the amount of light present, the focus of the lens, and the length of time the shutter is open all affect the resulting photograph.

> FUN FACT – The term *camera* comes from the Latin word for "vaulted room." The first camera was called a *camera obscura*, meaning "dark room," because it was originally a very large box. Thinking of a camera as a room, then, should also explain why the device that opens and closes the lens (the camera's "window") is called the shutter.

The following are all terms associated with photography and its variables:

The shutter speed determines how long the shutter remains open while taking a photograph. Light is captured on the sensor for the entire period the shutter is open, so a very quick shutter speed results in the capture of a split-second in time, a normal photograph. A much slower shutter speed captures all of the light during the open period. So, for example, if the shutter was open for the three seconds a leaf fell, the leaf's movement would be captured in the still photo, showing a blurred image of the leaf's progress during those three seconds. Many photographers call this timeframe the sensor's *exposure* to light. However as we'll see next, the term "exposure" also refers to the photograph itself. Because this overview is so brief, to avoid any confusion, I will only use the term "exposure" to indicate the photo quality described next.

Exposure describes the darkness or lightness of a photograph. Underexposed photos are generally dark while overexposed ones are too light.

Depth of field determines the distinct area within a photograph that appears in focus. Some photographs have the depth of field set so the foreground is in sharp focus, while the background is soft focused. Other have the reverse. Some photos have a sharp focus throughout. The depth of field is determined by the lens, the aperture, and the distance from the target.

An ISO speed is the camera's sensitivity to light. An ISO of 100 is considered low and works well when a lot of light is present, such as in daylight. A much higher ISO, such as 3200, means the camera is extremely sensitive to light and can take better photos in darker settings.

The <u>aperture</u> is the size of the opening in the lens, which determines how much light will be captured. The size is measured in <u>f-stops</u>. The smaller the f-stop, the more light is allowed on the sensor.

ACCURACY – Remember: just because photos exist doesn't mean they are accurate or interpreted correctly. Depending on your story, each of the above factors presents opportunities for fictional deception, collusion, and falsification of a scene. The darkness of an environment, the speed of an object, the time of day, and even the distance between objects can create potential rug-pulls and roadblocks for your investigators, perpetrators, and bystanders, innocent or otherwise.

Photographing the Scene

The entire purpose of photographing the scene is to show what was there without having others be physically present. Therefore, the photographs need to tell the story of the scene clearly, without confusion or misrepresentation.

Let's look back at the JonBenét Ramsey case; a full representation of the crime scene was never photographed. What the case ended up with was a few photos that barely related to each other. There was no way to reconstruct the scene. So, for example, when the Boulder Police Department claimed there were no footprints in the snow to suggest an intruder entered the broken window, the only exterior shot—which did not show the area around the window—showed a snow-free sidewalk and actually worked against their case. **Global shots** of the crime scene are essential. These are photographs that capture the entire area as it appears to someone approaching the scene on foot. If the area is too vast to capture in one shot, overlapping shots are taken. The goal is to capture the entire scene from a distance. If the target scene is a building, outside shots of the building should be taken as well as shots encompassing each individual room in its entirety. The objective is not to have these shots show what's of interest within a scene, such as a body or a piece of evidence, but to put the person viewing the photographs in the scene by showing its overall environment.

Additionally, each piece of evidence needs to be photographed. These shots tend to get tricky, as often investigators can forget the significance of a photo months or years after its creation. If the person viewing the photograph is unclear what it depicts or why the photographer took the shot, the photograph has not done its job. To avoid this, a crime scene photographer follows a strict methodology for every piece of evidence photographed.

> ACCURACY: You can make your scene photographer have a tremendous impact on the story by having him rush, cut corners, or not capture the entire scene.

The photographer covers everything that the lead

investigator wants photographed in three stages: overall, mid-range, and close-up. Put together, this series of photos takes the viewer into the scene and straight to the evidence, recording a coherent visual progression for later reference. This way the viewer knows exactly where the evidence is located and why it's important.

The first step is to establish the overall area. Much like the global pictures described above, these **overall shots** give the viewer the sense of the general location of the evidence by showing the entire significant area, be it a field off the highway, a front yard, or a particular room in a residence. This overall shot must include where the target evidence is located, even if the evidence itself is not discernible in the photo.

The next stage is called a **mid-range shot**, in which the photographer moves closer to show the evidence and the area around it. If the overall shot showed a utility pole in a field, the mid-range shot would be nearer to the pole and show the body at its base. If the overall shot was the guest bedroom, the mid-range shot would close in on the top side of the bed with the blood spatter on the wall above it. The goal is to show what's important in this series of shots (the evidence) while still showing where it's located in relation to the items visible around it.

Finally, the photographer takes the **close-up shots**, which are focused completely on the evidence and nothing else. Keeping with the above two examples, the close-up shots for those cases would be the photos depicting only the body in the field, and the pictures of the individual blood drips within the spatter pattern on the bedroom wall. Several close-up shots are taken of the evidence to get different angles and to ensure an acceptable picture. The photographer will also take shots with and without a ruler to convey scale.

> **PROCEDURE** – The photographer takes several photographs for every piece of evidence, including overall, mid-range and close-up shots.

The significance of this series of photographs is the clarity they bring after the fact. Too often a single close-up shot cannot express where that piece of evidence is specifically located, while a mid-range shot cannot give the necessary detail a close-up photo provides. Investigators can all too easily leap to a conclusion based on a misleading photo and an entire case can be cracked by a perfect series of shots that memorializes an overlooked detail everyone missed during the initial response.

Crime Scene Photography Techniques

Many obstacles impede the acquisition and accuracy of crime scene photos. The photographer does not get to choose the locale, the weather, or the time of day.

Sometimes the evidence is incredibly small, sometimes the environment around the evidence has competing colors, and sometimes the area is just too dark or bright for a satisfactory picture. Several specialized techniques are incorporated into the photographer's skill set to offset these difficulties.

Photo Scales

Specialized photography rulers, officially called **photomacrographic scales**, or photo scales for short, are used to represent relative size and to adequately adjust for camera positioning and accurate color.

> TERMS – Photomacrograph is the word for a photograph depicting the target at its actual size relative to its surroundings. A photomacrographic scale (aka photo scale) is used by photographers to determine the camera is in no way pitched or otherwise off when representing accurate crime scene photos.

The typical crime scene photo scale is two rulers joined at a 90-degree angle. As with all rulers, there are measurements on the inside of both arms. At the middle intersection, as well as at the end of each ruler, there are circles divided into quarters. These circles enable the photographer to ensure the photograph is taken from directly head-on, with no pitch in the camera angle. Many scales also have colored points that the developer could reference to make sure the printed color is true to the actual color.

Digital photography has taken away much of the color concerns of film photography.

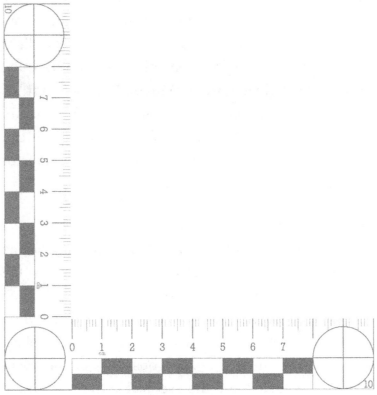

Figure 15: Photo Scale

Exposure Bracketing

Another significant issue with film photography, which has all but been corrected with digital cameras, is the concern the photo's exposure is off.

Having an overexposed or underexposed photo could prevent the picture from accurately representing the target of the photo. In the past, crime scene photographers who used film implemented a technique of exposure bracketing in which they took each important photo, such as the close-up shot of the evidence, several times with adjustments in the f-stop, increasing and decreasing the amount of light allowed in. By doing this, one photo should have the appropriate light exposure. With digital photography, however, the photographer can view the picture immediately after taking the shot. This way he can instantly evaluate the exposure and compensate for the light only when necessary.

Black and White

In many busy backgrounds, such as a forest floor, the colors and textures depicted can overwhelm the evidence itself, making it hard to see. One technique to counter this is simply taking a black and white photo of the evidence. Two things happen in black and white pictures. First, the busyness of the background is negated and the eye is able to focus on the photo's target. Second, shadows are enhanced, which gives the photo a clarity and contrast that was previously missing. Many overlooked details can be discovered by simply taking a black and white photo.

> PROCEDURE: A black and white picture will subdue the overwhelming details of a busy background and make the photo's target stand out with crisp specificity.

Painting with Light

Painting with light is a flash photography technique that is used in dark, large areas, such as an outdoor scene at night. When done correctly, the picture will show the scene completely lit up, without shadow or poor visibility. To understand how this works, let's first discuss how non-law enforcement photographers use this technique.

Remember that a camera's shutter speed determines how much time is captured on the picture. When the photographer sets the camera for a relatively slow shutter speed, the picture captures everything that happens in the target area while the shutter is open.

At normal, quick speeds, if a person walks into the target area during the picture, the photo shows the person in that one spot, only capturing the moment of time the shutter was opened. The picture's been photobombed. But if that same person were to walk through the area during an extended capture time, the picture would show that person's position throughout the entire area, for as long as the shutter was open, creating a blurred or "super speed" impression. The sensor will capture every place that person was while the shutter was opened, and it will all be captured on the picture. Likewise, as discussed previously, and seen in the following figure, a normal, quick shutter speed captures a falling leaf at a clear, single moment in time, while a slower shutter speed shows a blurred leaf, capturing every position of its movement while the shutter was open.

Fast Shutter Speed   **Slower Shutter Speed**

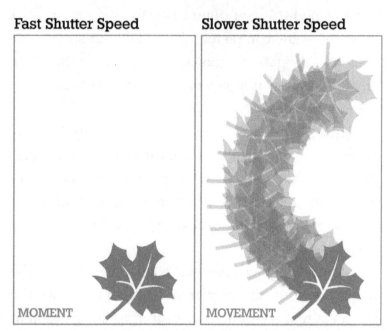

Figure 16: Comparing Fast to Slow Shutter Speeds

The same concept is true for light. If a flashlight is used in a dark area, the picture will only show the specific area the light was pointed toward at normal shutter speeds. However, if the shutter remains open, the flashlight can be redirected throughout the scene. Every area illuminated by the flashlight is added to the overall picture until the shutter is again closed.

Think of sparklers from the Fourth of July. Kids love to write their names in the air using the sparkler because our eyes can make out the letters of light as they are drawn. With sparklers, we typically see only one letter (or portion of a letter) at a time, but our eyes can see the light in the shapes that the kids are drawing. It's the same result with painting with light photography, except in this case, the picture can capture much more than our naked eye can.

On a dark night, when the shutter is kept open, if a person traced the outline of the side of a house with a flashlight, all that would show on the picture is the house's outline. Wherever the light goes during the time the shutter records the scene on the sensor is captured on the picture. So the subject is literally *painting* with the light.

The same concept is used during crime scene photography in dark areas, except instead of painting sections with light or creating shapes with the light, the goal here is to illuminate the entire scene and remove all of the darkness. I'm going to simplify this greatly for this text, but the resulting photograph is perfectly lit.

> TERMS – Painting with light, when used in a crime scene setting, creates a complete lighted photograph, even though the target is shrouded in darkness.

For this technique, the camera must have the shutter open for the entire process, which can be quite lengthy. Having the shutter open for that long requires it to be secured on a tripod. Any shaking or movement will distort the resulting image significantly. Essentially, a flash for the camera is used throughout the entire scene, illuminating different sections at a time.

The first position for the flash is determined beforehand and the flash is prepped. Then the shutter is opened and the flash is deployed. Then black cardboard is placed over the shutter and the flash is repositioned deeper into the target area. The cardboard prevents anything from being recorded except the scene when lit by the flash. There is a high risk of one of the investigators getting within the frame while repositioning the flash, and you don't want that in the picture. The cardboard keeps that investigator from being recorded. Also, since the shutter is covered by the cardboard and nothing can be recorded on the lens, other lights can be turned on to help reposition the flash. Once the cardboard is removed, however, the flash must be the only light.

When set, the cardboard is lowered, the flash is deployed and the cardboard is again used to cover the lens. This process continues until the flash has been positioned to cover the entire area, facing in from both sides of the frame so no shadows are left. This can take anywhere from six to twelve flashes, depending on the size of the area. In reality there is a bit of math involved and each flash position is calculated for the greatest effect, but that's too involved for the basic explanation I want to provide here. The goal of painting with light is a crime scene picture that is completely lit, devoid of all shadows.

Photo Log

An additional requirement in crime scene photography is the creation of a photo log. Too many examples exist of investigators going through the case photos several months into the investigation and coming across several in which they have no idea what they're looking at or why they took the picture. Now, with digital photography, where the sheer number of photos is significantly greater, the risk of forgetting the intended subject of certain specific shots is huge.

For this reason, a photo log is a required document that accompanies the complete set of crime scene photos. A **photo log** is simply a list that describes each picture at the time it was taken. The policy dictating what exactly needs to be annotated on a photo log varies agency to agency, but at a minimum, it includes the date of the photo, where the photo was taken (if the lead investigator segmented the scene into different search areas, for example), and a description of what the photographer was attempting to capture. The photos are numbered on the list, so that the 123rd photo will be line number 123 on the log. Other details, such as time, compass direction, and camera settings (aperture settings, flash, ISO if appropriate, etc.), are also recorded.

> TERMS – A photo log is a list of every photograph taken at the scene, in numerical order, that details what each photo depicts.

A significant question posed to crime scene photographers is whether they are ever allowed to delete photos, especially since the process is so easy with digital photography. Many old-schoolers will argue that no photo taken at a crime scene should ever be deleted for any reason at any time. But with technology now allowing us to instantly review photos so that they can be retaken if necessary, that philosophy doesn't always have to prevail. The photo log is created to annotate every crime scene photo and provide a file of what was recorded at that scene. However, since a photographer can now immediately evaluate a photograph, if that photograph does not do the job he hoped it would, there is no problem deleting it prior to filling out the log and retaking the shot. However, once that photo is put in the log, which is required once it's acceptable, that photo should never be deleted. So if the photographer reviews the photo in the picture viewer on the camera and decides the lighting was off, or his hands were shaking, or something else went wrong, he can delete that photo and retake it. When he is pleased with the photo, he logs it and moves onto the next one.

> **PROCEDURE** – Now that technology makes deleting pho-
> tographs from memory cards so easy, the photo log
> becomes incredibly important. Once a picture is entered
> on that list, should it ever end up missing from the investi-
> gation's photospread, an investigator's integrity is up for
> scrutiny and the entire case may be undermined.

Often the crime scene photographer creates his own photo log, but if the investigation can spare personnel, sometimes another officer is assigned to the photographer to fill out the log instead. This makes the process a bit more efficient as the photographer can concentrate on each shot without stopping every time to fill in the next line of the log. He need only speak aloud to his logger so she can write down the appropriate information for him.

There is obviously a lot that goes into crime scene photography and we really only touched on the topic here. Hopefully you can see several instances where you can exploit the strengths and weaknesses of crime scene photography for creative opportunities to add fascinating complexities to your books.

- A complete photographic coverage of the scene was never accomplished (think JonBenét Ramsey).
- The series method of overall, mid-range, close-up photographs for every piece of evidence was not followed. A single close-up photo can lead to confusion concerning where the target

is located or why it is important.

- The photos do not match up with the photo log. A photo is missing that is on the list or vice versa.
- One or several photographs indicate digital manipulation.
- A significant detail is captured in a photo that the on-scene investigators did not notice.

Videography

Not all law enforcement agencies agree on whether to make a video recording of the crime scene. Some agencies feel the liability outweighs the benefit, while others conclude in this age when private citizens create their own videos daily for social media posts, a jury of such citizens expects a video representation of the scene. Still other agencies leave the decision about whether to shoot a video up to the lead investigator.

One negative often cited about making a video of the scene is it forces a visual perspective. A juror can study a photograph, but a video includes movement. The video may not rest on a point of interest long enough, or conversely, may linger too long. Also, a viewer who expects the video to pan to the left may be a bit disoriented if it instead pans right. Further, while separate photos can be used to build a scene, the video shows an area at the videographer's height before it can go back and show the same area's ground/floor or overhead/ceiling. Videos taken by filmmakers who take the time to show the ground and overhead at every point in the scene during the time the video is going through it become tedious and unsettling.

Perhaps the biggest complaint against filming a crime scene is the audio. A law enforcement crime scene video should never include audio for two reasons:

First, any comments made by the videographer can come into question during court proceedings as biased or leading. The entire video may by challenged if either the prosecution or defense argue the audio attempts to sway a viewer to certain conclusions, especially when the viewer is a presiding judge or juror.

Second, law enforcement officials often use humor to deflect the seriousness of the crimes they are investigating. Investigators cannot later edit out any inappropriate or ill-timed comment caught on the video, and that comment will be available for scrutiny. Attorneys can use inappropriate comments to bring the officer's professionalism, and therefore competence, into question.

However, as noted above, many juries expect a video and as a result many departments film the scene as a means of easily showing the layout.

> **PROCEDURE** – Many law enforcement agencies disagree on whether the pros outweigh the cons for video use at a crime scene.

If you decide to use a crime scene video in your story, you can use any of the above drawbacks to complicate it.

- The video is difficult to watch because of an unsteady hand or awkward pans.
- The video does not cover the entire scene.
- The video stops just short of or speeds past a critical element or detail.
- The video reveals a completely overlooked detail or individual at the margins of a search or the scene's perimeter.
- The video shows investigators at work, which could mean it shows them cutting corners or using a technique incorrectly.
- The video recorded audio that captures conversations the investigators would rather not be publicized.

In the last several chapters we have discussed the difficulties associated with processing and recording the crime scene. Unfortunately, life rarely keeps things normal, especially in emergency situations. In the next chapter, we'll address some of the complexities officers have to face at various difficult scenes.

Chapter 5: Crime Scene Complications

Now that we've discussed the procedures for processing a crime scene, we need to address common complexities that present themselves when dealing with actual scenes. The lead investigator needs to be able to work around any complication and maintain as much scene integrity as possible.

Private Investigators

From Sherlock Holmes to Jessica Jones, private investigators are some of the most popular characters in fiction, hired to unearth forgotten details and crack the crimes the police cannot. Unfortunately, the unrestricted access and unconventional techniques of these fictional snoops are not strictly realistic. A private investigator, also called a PI, a private eye, or a private detective, is an individual who performs investigatory tasks for a fee. Often these investigations are not into matters that are criminal in nature, or do not reach a level of illegality for the police to be involved, as with adultery, for example.

FUN FACT – The terms "private detective" and "private investigator" are interchangeable, however many professional organizations prefer using "private investigator." This shift away from "private detective" is because many officials believe it's too easily confused with "police detective," which is a completely different individual, with different authority and access.

Private investigators are not law enforcement, and as such do not have the authority or limitations the police have. PIs cannot make official arrests, request or execute search warrants, or enforce any law. Likewise, the Fourth Amendment of the US Constitution does not apply to them, since they do not work for the government. For all intents and purposes, PIs, although required to be licensed, are private citizens, and are bound by the same laws as the rest of the populace. As a result, a PI cannot break into a person's house or business to search their files or collect significant evidence. Although the PI is not bound to honor a person's right to privacy granted by the Fourth Amendment, an overeager private detective committing the crimes of breaking and entering and trespassing can be arrested like any other citizen.

ACCURACY – Private investigators must be licensed through the state they work in. However, licensing requirements vary tremendously state to state. In Idaho, it's as simple as obtaining a business license. On the other end of the spectrum, in Virginia, a private investigator must meet a considerable training requirement, have endorsements, and submit to criminal background checks.

Unlike the crime-solving sleuths on television, real-world private investigators tend to be involved in issues of the private sector, including civil fraud matters, matrimonial discord, and locating witnesses. There are times, however, that lawyers on a criminal case, either the prosecution or the defense, may hire a PI to supplement or poke holes in the law enforcement investigation; the district attorney's office in the JonBenét Ramsey case hired an independent investigator when they did not agree with the Boulder Police Department's focus or findings. In these situations, the hiring agency provides the information needed by the PI to help kick-start their efforts. So although a PI would not be given full access to the law enforcement investigation, working side-by-side with the police, he would still be able to review anything the police provided to the lawyers.

As far as crime scenes go, the PI operates as a private citizen. If, as in many stories, the snoopy PI gets to the crime scene before the police turn up (and it's in a public space), he can do all the detecting he can, as could any other person. Once the police arrive, however, first responders will move the PI outside the perimeter with the other civilians. The lead investigator can decide if she thinks the PI's involvement is of any benefit, but realistically, she will probably only take note of any information he has to give before proceeding without his aid.

> **FUN FACT** – Whether you're a fan of the *Rockford Files*, *Magnum, P.I.*, or *Psych*, the popularization of the private detective in crime fiction can be traced back to Edgar Allan Poe. In his "The Murders in the Rue Morgue," Poe introduces C. Auguste Dupin, an amateur sleuth who solves a double homicide in Paris. Dupin also appears in "The Mystery of Marie Rogêt" and "The Purloined Letter."

Outdoor Scenes

Outdoor crime scenes bring with them many more difficulties when trying to preserve scene integrity because of environmental factors. Weather, terrain, and animal activity are all additional concerns beyond just Locard's Exchange Principle. The investigator's goal at any crime scene is to keep it pristine, or as unchanged as possible from the time the crime was committed. Often outdoor scenes make this impractical.

Rain can literally wash evidence away, while a heavy snowstorm can hide it until a thaw. High temperatures can degrade certain evidence at an accelerated rate. High winds can damage or cover evidence such as footprints, tire tracks, or finger-prints.

Mudslides or sandy scenes can make transporting equipment dangerous. Mountainous areas may make part of the scene inaccessible. An area of dense foliage can mask evidence that has fallen to the ground below it.

Many animals are attracted to remains or bodily fluids. Flies, beetles, and carnivorous mammals feed off of bodies, destroying evidence and altering the remains available for evaluation. Larger predators are known to carry the remains off to a totally unrelated area, altering the scene and leaving evidence that has nothing to do with the perpetrator.

Investigators deal with these added complications as best they can. Perhaps they raise tarps to try and protect areas from rain or snow. Maybe the lead investigator calls for a rushed search that moves any evidence to a climate-controlled building for appro-priate processing in order to beat a heavy snowstorm or to minimize the damage caused by high tempera-ture. Maybe a helicopter is the best option to cross dangerous terrain. Bottom line: the lead investigator needs to take every obstacle into account and form a plan to deal with it.

Water Scenes

A common misconception is that items found in

water have lost their evidentiary value. Sometimes this is true, or at least the value has been greatly diminished. However, there are several documented cases of retrieving valuable submerged evidence. Investigators have recovered fingerprints, trace evidence, and even DNA from underwater searches. The recovery process carries a risk of washing away or destroying this evidence, but the potential for searchers to find significant evidence exists. Some of the techniques used by law enforcement to collect the evidence require adjustment for the water environment, but dumping evidence in a river or overboard while at sea does not automatically give the culprit a free pass.

A submerged environment brings its own dangers and complications. For this reason, many agencies have their own trained teams of specialized divers. As with the processing procedures on land, a lead diver takes charge of the team, and they process the scene methodically, marking the evidence as they find it.

> **PITFALL** – Underwater conditions are considered danger-ous, even in calm, clear environments. An agency will not put itself at risk by sending its normal crime scene investi-gators into the water. A fully trained and certified crime scene diving team is required.

A difference exists in the size of the team, as there are fewer certified divers than responding investigators. Also, these are not controlled, recreational dives, and the divers enter dangerous currents and areas of low-to-no visibility. For this reason, every diver works while tethered and has an assigned line tender on the surface whose job is to continuously monitor the tether.

Investigators do not mark this evidence with the typical evidence markers, but use buoys instead. This way, when the evidence is ready for collection, the diver can head directly to the spot on the surface and dive straight down to it. The buoys also provide a visible layout of locations for the investigators on the surface.

Specialized diving equipment, from lights to cameras to collection materials can be expensive and require additional training. However, if an agency has a fully equipped, certified team, water scenes can provide a case with significant evidence.

Multiple Scenes

Sometimes a criminal act has more than one crime scene. The lead investigator needs to be prepared to send officers to respond and process the other scenes as they are identified. Multiple-scene cases involve several considerations.

The lead investigator is still in charge of the investigation and makes all decisions. She needs to coordinate the team that will respond to the new scene. There will be one investigator at the new scene who will take charge, but that investigator will still report to the lead investigator. Coordinating multiple scenes makes frequent and clear communication essential and greatly increases the need for a command post at the original scene.

Investigators refer to the first crime scene as the **primary scene**, while all others are called **secondary scenes**. The first scene is where all of the focus began and where the lead investigator is located. For her to try to designate which scene is primary based on its importance every time a new scene is identified is both unnecessary and inefficient. All scenes should be processed the same way, so importance does not matter, and relocating to another scene just because its designation has changed is a waste of time. The first scene is the primary scene and every additional scene is a secondary scene. If the initial call was the discovery of a body, that area is the primary scene. The place the murder happened and the vehicle used to transport the body are secondary scenes.

TERMS – A primary scene is the first scene investigators respond to, not necessarily the scene where the crime occurred. Every additional scene is called a secondary scene.

As mentioned, secondary scenes are processed in the exact same manner that the primary scene is. A perimeter is established, photographs are taken, a sketch is drawn, and a methodical search pattern is followed to identify evidence.

There are many issues to consider when a secondary scene is identified.

- Is an immediate response required? If so, who will make up that team?
- Are the legal search exceptions still valid, or is a search warrant required?
- Is there a change in geographical jurisdiction? Even if the location of the secondary scene should change the jurisdiction, most law enforcement agencies respect an ongoing investigation and either allow the original investigators to handle the scene or work in conjunction with them.

> **PITFALL** – Although the law enforcement community extends respect to an original officer from a different jurisdiction so he can participate on a secondary scene, the same does not apply to an unrelated crime scene. In other words, the car used in a murder that is located across state lines is a secondary scene. A completely different murder is not.

Probably the biggest concern for a case when it comes to multiple scenes is the concept of cross-contamination. It is something that every law enforcement official who works crime scenes needs to be constantly aware of. **Cross-contamination** is a relocation of evidence from one crime scene onto another, which then creates a false link between the two scenes.

Remember the evidence triangle? The entire reason to search a crime scene is to find evidence, and the job of evidence is to connect the suspect, victim, and scene to each other. If one or more of those links are invalid, the case cannot be proven. That scene is now cross-contaminated.

> TERMS – Cross-contamination is the transfer of evidence between scenes or onto objects not previously containing that evidence. It creates a false link between the objects.

Cross-contamination can certainly be done on purpose, by an officer with malicious intent (which is referred to as planting evidence or framing the suspect). However, the vast majority of cross-contamination incidents are not done intentionally or with any awareness it even occurred. They are simply the result of sloppy scene processing.

For example, consider a scene where the investigator is handling bloody weapons or processing blood on a wall. The investigator may inadvertently get blood on his sleeve. If that investigator is then sent to a secondary scene, such as the suspect's discovered vehicle, and again without realizing it, brushes that sleeve on the car, that vehicle has been cross-contaminated with the victim's blood. Think of how strong that evidence becomes once it's discovered. The victim's blood on the suspect's car provides a powerful connection. The link is so strong that it may be enough to convict the suspect of being involved in the victim's death. But that evidence should never have been there. It was an invalid link. Further, if cross-contamination is suspected, the questioned evidence can no longer be considered. The risk that it provides a false link, even if the reality is it was not cross-contaminated, is too great. This is why cross-contamination becomes a huge concern in investigations.

> PITFALL – Having your main character jump scene to scene opens up the entire investigation to cross-contamination allegations.

There are a couple of ways to combat cross-contamination, and in doing so, to validate the links in the evidence triangle. The easiest policy is to prohibit anyone at one scene from visiting any other scene. If no investigator can deposit the unsuspected evidence he's carrying, no link can be made. This is not very realistic, however, as most law enforcement agencies face budgetary and personnel limitations. Few departments have enough available investigators to have two completely separate teams.

Another protection against cross-contamination is to completely change an investigator's outer clothing before entering a different scene. The easiest way to do this is to ensure every investigator is wearing PPE while processing a scene. As stated previously, PPE protects an officer from any biohazards in a scene, but just as significantly, it also protects the scene from the investigator. Should the officer inadvertently get evidence on himself, like with the blood in the above example, he cannot redeposit it elsewhere because he completely removed all of the disposable PPE at the first scene and dressed again in sterile PPE at the next scene. No evidence ever leaves its scene.

False Scenes

False scenes are crime scenes that are altered by the addition, removal, or moving of evidence in an attempt to misdirect investigators. The process is called "staging the scene." A distinction should be made between staging the scene and cleaning or covering up the scene. The purpose of staging the scene is to alter what's found there to intentionally send the investigation in the wrong direction. Someone who cleans or covers up a scene hopes to simply stump investigators by taking away the evidence that may lead to him; he's not necessarily sending the officers in a wrong direction. Staging takes planning and malicious intent, while cleaning a scene could be seen simply as panic and self-preservation.

> **TERMS** – Staging is a purposeful act to alter a crime scene by adding, removing, or moving evidence with the explicit intention of misdirecting an investigation.

Arson is an act that could be used in either situation. If the suspect is simply burning what's there so nothing can lead back to him, he's covering up the scene with the fire. However, if he is attempting to use the arson to convince investigators that an accidental fire from faulty wiring was what caused the death, that's staging. It's the *purposeful misdirection* that is the key distinguisher.

Staging a false scene can be something simple or incredibly interwoven and complex, depending on how much planning and preparation the culprit spent on it.

In 1970, Dr. Jeffrey MacDonald killed his pregnant wife and two young daughters and then tried to claim hippies had invaded his home. He turned over the coffee table and one potted plant in the living room to prove there had been a struggle, and planted the word "pig" written in blood on the master bedroom headboard. This minimal staging failed to convince the Army investigators, and MacDonald was arrested for the murders.

The most important thing any lead investigator or scene searcher can do when arriving at a crime scene is to let the evidence tell the story. As mentioned in Chapter 3, investigators need to resist tunnel-vision and not force a scene to validate any preconceived or easy conclusions. No matter how much staging occurs, the suspect is going to overlook something or not realize the false scene does not make sense. Most stagings can be identified if a thorough, methodical search is conducted.

Crime Scene Cleaners

One crime scene topic people tend to forget or leave unaddressed is what happens after the processing ends. Once the lead investigator releases the scene, who's left to clean it up? Unfortunately, we don't have magic wands or adorable talking mice to spiff everything up in a jiffy.

Crime scene clean-up typically falls to private businesses specifically created for that purpose. Hundreds of companies explicitly offer cleaning services to decontaminate and sterilize sites containing potential biohazard materials and remove clutter or damage. They even utilize ozone purifiers to remove any unpleasant odors.

Some states require certification for crime scene cleaners that comply with OSHA and EPA standards; some require licensing for medical waste transport. Because of these businesses' expertise, many crime scene cleaners also attend to sites involving hoarders or commercial medical/hazardous waste.

In many cases, homeowner's or business insurance will cover the cost of the clean-up, but several cities have laws that require the public services of either the police or fire department to pay the bill from their budget. Do some digging to determine how this is handled in the location of your story.

> PROCEDURE – Crime scene cleaners are private companies hired to clean up the mess after the crime scene is released. It's the perfect job cover to get private eye or snooping cozy mystery characters onto your scene.

If you need to find a way to get a fictional amateur sleuth onto a scene, consider having him work as a crime scene cleaner. Any overlooked evidence or encounters with reluctant witnesses can open up fascinating possibilities for characters outside the investigative community!

Case Study #2: O.J. Simpson – How Cross-Contamination Can Topple a Mountain of Evidence

The O.J. Simpson court case was referred to as the Trial of the Century and at the time received unequaled media attention. It maintained top news coverage from every station, and for outlets like CNN, Headline News, and Court TV, it dominated their programming. The outcome shocked most of the world, with many at-home spectators outraged. The case remains a perfect glimpse into America's legal system, and it's one of the reasons I stress so often in this book the importance of solid police work and properly processed crime scenes.

This case, like every other court proceeding in this country, came down to the evidence. Criminal cases in the United States have a higher standard of proof than civil or small claims cases. *Beyond a reasonable doubt* means that the evidence submitted for the case must be strong enough that no other rational explanation exists. The defendant is found guilty by a court because the evidence establishes that guilt beyond a reasonable doubt. If the evidence fails to meet that standard, then the defendant *must* be found not guilty of the crime. This is to protect a fundamental right given to all American citizens: every American is considered innocent until *proven* guilty.

When evidence is not collected correctly or mishandled in some way, the validity of that evidence comes into question. That is why the integrity of the crime scene is vitally important at the very outset of a criminal investigation, and why the threat of cross-contamination can destroy a case. Both of these concepts played a pivotal role in the outcome of the O.J. Simpson trial. The prosecutors thought they had insurmountable evidence that proved what happened, but as the defense attorneys punched holes in each and every piece, they raised enough reasonable doubt to set O.J. free.

BACKGROUND

Nicole Brown Simpson had been married to O.J. for seven years before they divorced. The couple had two children. Their relationship had been turbulent and O.J. had pleaded no contest to spousal abuse while they were married. At the time of her death, Nicole and O.J. had just begun attempting to reconcile their relationship.

Ron Goldman was a recent friend of Nicole's and worked as a waiter at a restaurant she frequented. They went out several times, but never claimed to be in a relationship. On the night of the murders, Nicole called Ron's work to report her mother had left her sunglasses there. Ron offered to bring the sunglasses to Nicole after his shift ended.

THE EVIDENCE

At approximately 9:30–11:00 PM on June 12, 1994, Nicole and Ron were murdered just inside the gate to Nicole's townhome complex. The evidence at the scene conveyed that the assailant incapacitated Nicole and then murdered Ron before turning back and killing her. A black knit hat and leather glove found near Ron's body suggested the assailant lost his hat during the struggle, took off his gloves in an attempt to find it in the dark, and was spooked, leaving the hat and one glove behind. Although the door to Nicole's home was open, there was no indication of trespassing or burglary.

The evidence placing O.J. at the murder (primary) scene was overwhelming:

- Neighbor Jill Shively reported she saw O.J. speeding away from the scene in his white Bronco around the time of the murders.
- Hairs found in the knit cap matched O.J.'s .
- Fibers on the knit cap matched material in O.J.'s white Bronco.
- A size-12 Bruno Magli shoeprint was found at the primary scene. O.J. was proven to own a

pair of size-12 Bruno Magli shoes.

- DNA tests proved that three blood stains found on the gate to Nicole's condominium belonged to O.J.
- DNA tests proved that five blood drops found near the footprints belonged to O.J.
- Hairs found on Ron's shirt matched O.J. 's.
- Fibers found on Ron's shirt matched the material of the sweat suit O.J. 's houseguest, Kato Kaelin, reported seeing O.J. wearing that night.

As investigators began honing in on O.J. as a suspect, two secondary crime scenes were established: his white Ford Bronco and his home. The evidence continued mounting at those secondary scenes:

- Limo driver Allan Park reported he arrived at O.J. 's house at 10:40 PM to take him to the airport. He testified he buzzed the house from the gate but received no reply.
- Kaelin reported hearing three thumps outside the house at 10:50 PM.
- Park reported seeing a large black man walk through the yard and enter the front door of the house, turning on the lights at about that time. Park stated that he then buzzed the house again and O.J. immediately picked up, saying he had overslept.

- Kaelin and Park helped O.J. load five suitcases into the limo, but O.J. was adamant neither of them was to touch a small black bag.
- Park stated that on the way to the airport O.J. was visibly sweating and complained he was hot, although it was a cool night and the air conditioning was on.
- When police arrived, they noticed the white Bronco was parked haphazardly. They found blood on the door. DNA tests showed the blood was O.J. 's.
- DNA tests proved blood on the Bronco's console was a mixture of O.J. 's, Nicole's, and Ron's.
- DNA tests proved Nicole's blood was on the driver side carpet.
- Blood drops were found on the driveway and in the foyer of O.J. 's home. DNA tests showed it was O.J.'s blood.
- Blood was found on a pair of socks on the floor of O.J.'s bedroom. DNA tests proved the blood was both O.J. 's and Nicole's.
- A glove, found to be a match to the one left at the primary scene, was found outside O.J. 's home, near where Kaelin claimed to hear the thumps.
- DNA tests proved Ron's blood was on that glove.

- Fibers found on this glove matched the carpeting in O.J. 's white Bronco.
- Hairs found on this glove were consistent with both Nicole and Ron.
- After a warrant was issued for his arrest, O.J. failed to turn himself in at the agreed-upon time. He was later spotted driving in his white Bronco with Al Cowlings, which led to news outlets broadcasting a 90-minute slow-speed chase in real time.
- When O.J. was arrested he had four cuts and seven abrasions, the most serious being a severe cut on his left middle finger. When asked how he got that, O.J. changed his story three times, ultimately sticking with, "I don't know."

THE DEFENSE

The amount of evidence in this case was enormous. But at the end of the trial, it didn't matter. The defense took on a strategy that was more offense than defense. They didn't try to explain O.J.'s motivations or actions, but instead attacked the detectives and forensic specialists in an attempt to discredit each piece of evidence. A lack of crime scene integrity and adherence to policy proved to be this case's undoing.

Detective Mark Fuhrman was at the primary murder scene as well as the two secondary scenes. He was the detective who found the first glove, the blood on the Bronco, the second glove (at O.J.'s home), and the socks in O.J. 's bedroom. Not only was cross-contamination a threat with this evidence, but the defense took it a step further by implying Fuhrman purposely planted the evidence to frame O.J.

During the course of Fuhrman's testimony, the defense's goal was to discredit him, which they accomplished when they caught him in a lie on the stand (regarding how he referred to African Americans). Once Fuhrman's character was impeached, anything he contributed to the case became extremely questionable.

Detective Philip Vannatter faced similar intense examination by the defense. He was forced to admit he did not enter the blood taken from O.J. during their police interview into evidence immediately as required by policy. He admitted to bringing that blood to an active crime scene (O.J.'s house) so the forensic technician could enter it into the evidence log there.

Evidence from another scene (in this case O.J.'s body) should never have been introduced to a different, active scene (O.J.'s house). An accidental cross-contamination could result in making the links in the evidence triangle invalid.

The defense's farfetched claims that O.J. 's blood was planted at each of the scenes became much less improbable when Vannatter, one of the lead detectives, admitted carrying around a blood vial in his pocket. Once evidence is tainted by doubt, its value is greatly diminished. Once a crime scene is compromised, all remaining evidence in it (Nicole's and Ron's blood for example) is equally doubted. Once cross-contamination concerns become legitimized, the evidence loses most of its value.

Yet another on-scene witness, Forensic Expert Dennis Fung, spent nine days on the stand under extreme cross-examination. Under oath, Fung, whom the prosecution called to introduce all of the blood and DNA evidence, admitted to the defense attorneys that he did not follow strict collection and handling procedures when dealing with the blood from the scenes. He even admitted to not always wearing gloves while working at the sites, a blunder so basic that all of Fung's testimony regarding the strength of the DNA evidence became suspect. If an expert cannot be relied upon to follow the most fundamental practices, how can he be believed that he conducted adequate and reliable complicated procedures?

As stated above, in the United States, citizens are considered innocent until proven guilty. That means the defense did not have to prove O.J. innocent. All they had to do was produce a reasonable doubt regarding O.J.'s involvement. If the prosecution could not overcome that doubt, the jury had no choice but to find him not guilty. The defense did not focus on debunking a motive or giving O.J. an alibi. Sloppy police work and poor crime scene processing gave the defense their direction. All they had to do was introduce a question mark in the jurors' minds for each piece of evidence the prosecution presented. By discrediting the way the investigators processed the crime scenes and by introducing the possibility of cross-contamination, especially with purposeful and malicious intent, they succeeded in doing just that.

The entire defense case rested on challenging the validity of the evidence provided, and in doing so, allowed O.J. to be set free. Had the different crime scenes had integrity, where no investigator was on more than one scene, where no evidence from any scene was brought to any other, where procedure was followed and professionalism was unquestioned, the defense would have found their job an impossible climb. This case brought the dangers of cross-contamination, or more specifically the threat of using the possibility of cross-contamination as a defense, to a national spotlight. As a result, every law enforcement agency takes cross-contamination very seriously and trains their officers on how to protect against it. However, by not maintaining the sanctity of these scenes and by not following crime scene procedures, the investigators of this case handed the defense the unlikely win.

Chapter 6: Writing Your Crime Scene

Writing is hard. If I've learned anything from my years in and around the writing community, it's that. If you're not pouring out your soul, you're pulling out your hair, with very little time in-between. I believe that's why so many writing reference guides lean toward the "making it easy," "simple steps to..." pitch.

Solve Your Crime First

It may seem counterproductive, then, that in *Crime Scenes: Forensics for Fiction Series* I'm taking the opposite approach. When writing crime scenes, taking the road that is initially difficult leads to a much easier, organic conclusion. I always urge authors to adopt the tougher strategy of solving the crime before you commit it. Knowing how you will resolve everything helps tremendously in planting the seeds along the road to get there.

The most common draw for readers of fictional crime is, after a full story of bobs and weaves, the bad guy gets what's coming to him. Readers crave the satisfaction provided when crime is solved and order is restored. That means the crime has to be drawn out over the story, precluding the option for an open-and-shut case, solved at the primary crime scene.

In my years of reading crime fiction and later consulting with creators, I've learned that writing the crime scene *first*, and then proceeding through the investigation as the story is written, usually pins the author into an ugly corner.

Writing crime scenes can be exciting. Deciding how the evidence is misleading or covered up can flex the creative muscles and introduce juicy complications for your characters. However, too many times authors are caught in a dilemma: Now that I've made the crime so difficult to solve, how do I solve it? What is that one case-cracking piece of evidence that will lead us to the perpetrator no one's seen before? How can the evidence, that has been overlooked or misinterpreted for the entire story, suddenly become strong enough that it carries the weight I need it to? Too often, these questions can't be answered and the resulting wrap-ups contain logic leaps and shaky yet invariably convenient and spot-on conclusions.

> PITFALL – Avoid setting yourself up for logic leaps. Figure out the ending before diving into the crime scene.

When a writer takes the time to figure out how investigators first identify, then capture the suspect, writing the crime scene becomes much easier. The writer already has in mind what evidence needs to be obscure or lead characters down the wrong path, while knowing what true evidence must be present but unevaluated. Writing with a clear destination leads to a solid story. Making it up as you go along often requires significant backtracking to get back on course and wrap up with a satisfying finale.

So, what are some examples of that case-resolving piece of evidence? The answer depends only on your imagination. It just has to establish a strong enough evidence triangle link to avoid being a logic leap, and planned early enough in your writing preparation that it fits neatly into the story.

Crime Scene Menu

Once you've determined what evidence will lead to your perpetrator(s), then you're ready to plant it! Committing your crime should be the fun part, although some authors rush though details or get overwhelmed with the preparation it takes to do a credible job. To aid you in that endeavor, I've pre-pared a menu of questions which, when answered, will provide all the ingredients for the perfect crime scene for your investigators to tackle. Every story varies, so don't be surprised if every crime scene leads you to a different kind of investigation. The bonus is that every detail potentially adds depth, texture, and direction to your story.

SETTING: Is the scene…

- Inside/Outside/Combination/Multiple scenes?
- Rural/Suburban/Urban?
- Private/Public/Transitory?
- Open/Secure/Trespassed?
- Local/State/Federal Jurisdiction?
- Closed off/Easily accessible?

CONDITIONS: Is the environment…

- Climate controlled/Exposed to the elements?
- Rainy/Windy/Snowy/Foggy/Mild?
- Excessively hot/Extremely cold/Bearable?
- Arid/Humid/Comfortable?
- Sunny/Hazy/Dark at night/Artificially lit?

OBJECTS: What is in the scene?

- Landscaped or wild? Organized or cluttered?
- Trees? Dense foliage? Other vegetation?
- Concrete streets/Sidewalks? Carpeted/Hardwood/Tiled floors?
- Vehicles? Trash bins? Mailbox? Bus stop?
- Furniture? Lamps? Appliances?
- Linens and drapes?
- Toys/Clothes/Tools/Books?
- Weapons?

PEOPLE: Who is present for the crime? Who is/are…

- The perpetrator(s)?

- The victim(s)?
- The involved witnesses (those connected to the suspect or victim)?
- The peripheral witnesses (passersby/observers)? Seen or unseen?

CRIME: What happened? What's your crime?
- Assault?
  - Physical/sexual?
  - How violent? How much trauma and of what type?
  - What weapon (hand/glass/club/knife/sword/gun)?
  - What injuries (blunt force/sharp force/burn)?
- Murder?
  - What weapon?
  - Simple or overkill?
  - Intentional or accidental?
  - Disfigurement/dismemberment?
  - Concealment?
- Burglary?
  - Entry and exit points?
  - What was stolen?
  - Value or importance?
  - Ransacked/No visible search?
- Abduction?
  - Age, description, vulnerability of victim?
  - In the open/victim just missing?

- ○ Attacked or lured?
- ○ Signs of injury or struggle?
- ○ How was victim subdued?
- ○ Any demands?
- Arson?
  - ○ How was the fire started?
  - ○ What accelerants were used?
  - ○ Value of property damaged?
  - ○ Parties affected by the damage?
  - ○ Insurance claim/Cover up another crime/Pyromania?
- Vandalism?
  - ○ What was the target? What is its value and import?
  - ○ Was the purpose destruction/intimidation/pride?
  - ○ What was used (paint/club/key/knife)?
  - ○ Intentional or impulsive?

EVIDENCE: What evidence is found that…
- Leads to the suspect (what you determined when you solved your crime first)?
- Misdirects or redirects the investigators?
- Is overlooked/misunderstood/misplaced/misinterpreted?

INTERFERENCE: What intentional hardships exist in the scene? Does it have…

- Animal activity (wild or domesticated)?
- A loss of scene integrity (poor scene security)?
- Amateur sleuths? Would-be Samaritans? Official malfeasance/incompetence?
- Staging or cleanup by perpetrator?

Answering these questions fleshes out your entire crime scene, providing structure for your characters' actions and decisions. Focus on the specifics that become pivotal for progressing the story. You'll have all your decisions already mapped out. What will lead my characters to the solution? What are the red herrings? What is the perpetrator most/least afraid of, and how does either lead to his downfall? What evidence is misread and is either overhyped or disregarded by the law enforcement community or the media?

What's important with these questions is they highlight your roadmap on how to complicate the investigation. Look for the problems and wrong turns that will keep your readers on edge. An open-and-shut case does not make a book, so you need to find the vulnerabilities in the crime scene you just created. Having it laid out in front of you gives you the vantage point you need to steer a path through the puzzle.

Complicating Your Evidence

Once you know how to wrap up your caper and

which evidence you'll need to do it properly, how do you make that evidence not so obvious right off the bat? How can you delay the solution and keep a fascinating question mark hanging over your story for as long as necessary?

Probably the simplest method of complicating your crime scene is to **Locard the heck out of it**. We've discussed Locard's Exchange Principle often throughout this book; now you get to run with it. Locard said that any time anyone enters a scene, they change it. They leave part of themselves behind and take some of it with them.

The JonBenét Ramsey case showed so many instances where evidence could have been added to the body or taken from it. So many people were in that home and her father placed her body in the hallway where they all had been milling about. The on-scene detective then moved the body to the living room, where all of these visitors had been consoling the parents. Her father placed a non-sterile sheet over her body. These are perfect ways to get unrelated evidence onto a body or to take significant evidence off, intentionally or innocently.

Notice the potential for dramatic complication and compelling character choices. Just by looking at Locard's Principle, you can tie characters to a scene, a crime, and each other in ways that can be unpacked over the course of an entire story.

Pets are terrible for pristine crime scenes and live for Locard's Exchange Principle. They can destroy blood evidence by lying down in it, brushing up against it or (gross) licking it up. They can obscure footprints by walking over or lying on them. Their fur can cling to wet surfaces, covering blood on a wall or semen on a sheet. They can move things around, perhaps making some evidence appear to be not so vital, such as pulling a sheet into a corner to lie on.

Wild animals are often attracted to dead bodies outdoors. They can destroy evidence on the body by eating it. They can take evidence off of the scene completely. In one of my cases, after tearing a decomposing body apart, wolves removed much of it to a completely different location. The victim's skull and arm bones were found months later a significant distance away, where the wolves rested to enjoy their meal.

The most infuriating, and dare I say satisfying, evidence transfers always seem to come from the crime scene professionals themselves. This does not always have to be presented in the form of the bumbling cop or the crooked agent. Great officers can still make egregious mistakes. Remember, everybody who enters that scene changes it to some extent, and there are a lot of people on a crime scene. Many instances of mistakes or simple lack of focus can result in fascinating and galling complications.

Allowing your investigators to live and breathe and mess up occasionally makes them *feel* real while adding dimension to a crime scene.

When in doubt, let Locard's Principle serve as your Swiss army knife of crime scene creation.

Considerations for Fictional Crime Scenes

Over the course of this book we've discussed many different aspects of crime scenes, from who's there to what's done to why it's important. Unfortunately, stories often cannot perfectly mirror real life.

As an example, we covered just how many people can be at a crime scene. For both authors and readers of fiction, it's difficult to keep up with too many characters. Likewise, the main character needs to have access to everything from her POV, so she can pass it on to the reader. The issue becomes a balance between legitimate forensics and artistic license so that your story packs the right kind of wallop.

What shortcuts can an author take while still keeping an air of realism?

One technique used in most fiction is to fuse all of the different roles found at a crime scene into one person. Magically, this gives your protagonist the knowledge and authority to be involved with everything going on at once. She is the lead investigator, making all of the decisions but also personally completing the searches and conducting all the interviews. She can collect the fingerprints and evaluate the blood spatter. She has access to the laboratory and can conduct the necessary tests. This is not realistic at all, but makes a certain kind of narrative sense.

However, even with an amalgamated investigator, writers need to do enough research to answer several questions when it comes to their fictional crime scenes:

• Why is your character there?

Your character must be allowed to be on the scene you want her processing. In order to adequately show this, you must answer three sub-questions:

○ Does she have the <u>right</u> to be there?

This is where, as a writer, you need to identify the probable cause for law enforcement involvement. In the vast majority of stories, you can answer this simply: someone reported a crime. A call for suspected illegal activity is not only the definition of probable cause that a crime has occurred, it's the essential job description of law enforcement. However, just because this tends to be simple, do not overlook this question, just to be sure you've checked the box.

Remember, in crime scenes that occur during the course of an ongoing investigation, with no emergency aspect to them, investigators need to have a warrant to be on the premises, unless they have a recognized exception such as the owner granting consent. Warrants are not given out easily. The investigator must prove probable cause to a judge. If there is not reasonable certainty that specific evidence will be found for a specific crime at that specific location, the warrant will not be granted. And no matter what fifty years of cop shows and erotic thrillers would have us believe, hunches do not meet the probable cause standard.

○ **Does she have the <u>jurisdiction</u> to be there?**
Remember, jurisdiction covers the legal authority of an investigation. So, which agency is going to investigate this crime? Locally the jurisdiction is geographical: police handle cities and towns while sheriffs cover counties. State agencies are limited by their state borders, but can take certain investigations from the locals. Federal agencies tend to be limited by investigation type, and can also take investigations away from the locals, as well as state officers. Do a bit of research just to ensure the agency you have your investigator working for is the agency that would investigate that scene.

There are huge jurisdictional infractions in stories that have the officer visiting a different county or state. While there, she somehow gets involved with processing a nearby scene. Beware of investigators who blithely step on toes and waltz into cases anywhere in the world. Law enforcement is a job that operates within strict, clear boundaries.

This is a pet peeve of a lot of investigators who would otherwise enjoy mysteries and crime shows: flashing a badge does not automatically grant access. Know the limits of your characters' access and authority.

○ **Does she have the <u>duty</u> to be there?**

What job does your investigator have? If you've created an amalgamated position, this may be easy to answer: she has *all* the jobs. But if you're being strictly realistic, involving everyone who would normally be there, what specifically does your character do in her job? Is she the lead investigator? Is she a first responder? Is she the photographer? While for certain crime scenes it is possible for certain local offices to send everyone to assist, generally each agency only sends people in that specialized unit, depending on the departmental section's makeup. For example, if the office has a Missing Persons/Kidnapping unit in its Violent Crimes Section, those are the officers who would respond to a kidnapping. The homicide detectives would be doing their own casework.

If a federal agency takes jurisdiction, it is not unheard of for them to supplement their manpower from the local agency. However, this is typically for the grunt work, and once that's done, so is the local agency's involvement. This can set up animosity at times as the locals feel they do work that takes them from their own cases, yet they get none of the credit for the investigation. Can you imagine the possibilities for significant character conflict and escalation? This local/federal friction can produce intense rivalry, misdirection, and opportunities for drama if you do your homework and set it up correctly.

• Who is at the scene?

If your character is not a mix of everyone, who is there? The more complex or high-profile the case, the more people will be involved. Is there media? How are they handled? Did first responders arrive? How did they change the scene? Are there onlookers? Are they peaceful or anti-cop? Picture in your mind the size of the scene and start placing the people in and around it. Does it feel claustrophobic or vast? Is the chaos controlled or rampant? A list that reviews the typical crime scene personnel is provided below in the Quick Reference section.

• What complexities does the scene present? What logistics are required?

These may change for every scene you write, but if you include complexities, be sure your investigators address them. You cannot have a crime scene on a mountaintop without investigators figuring out how to get equipment there, dealing with the extreme conditions there or adjusting for specific challenges such as working on ground at a significant pitch. If an outdoor scene is in the dead of winter, a blizzard creates an urgency for rapid processing, which can lead to missed evidence. Specialized techniques require specialized training. Crime scene divers are required for underwater scenes, blood spatter experts evaluate patterns, coroners or medical examiners are mandatory for bodies and so on. Complications can produce fascinating story tensions.

Crime Scene by Genre

How do different genres affect your crime scene? Again, the answer depends on you, but let's consider situational options from a variety of genres.

Police Procedural

This genre, I would argue, gives us the most "normal" crime scenes, if such things actually exist in genre entertainment. I would place most of the popular cop shows, from *Hill Street Blues* to *Law & Order* to *NCIS* in this category. The crime scene is basically the story and you can easily use any of the complications we've discussed in this book.

- Who discovers the crime and how?
- What agencies respond to the call and how do they interact?
- What evidence is discovered or not? Concealed or not? Disturbed or not?
- Are the investigators following correct procedures?

- Is there cross-contamination?
- Is weather or terrain or political influences creating difficulty?

Thriller

From a forensic perspective, I would classify these stories as amped-up police procedurals. In these stories the stakes are typically higher and the clock is definitely ticking. Unlike mysteries, we often meet the perpetrator long before law enforcement does. The tension is not in the *whodunit*, but rather in the *can-they-get-away-with-it*?

- Are the investigators outclassed by the expert assailant?
- Has the assailant staged the scene to throw them off?
- Are the assailant's weapons more sophisticated or higher quality than what the cops are used to dealing with on the street?
- Does the scene have to be processed quickly because of a present danger?
- Does that introduce sloppiness or missed evidence?
- With the heightened stakes typical to thrillers, how are the crime scenes situated, complicated, and addressed coherently?
- How does the crime scene contribute to the perpetrator's odds of success?

Historical

Historicals make for fun forensics because the crime scenes rely more heavily on the wit and smarts of the investigator than on our comfy technological advances of today.

- Is your time period prior to fingerprint analysis, scientific expertise, or public records?
- What kind of law enforcement and public protection exists? How do the laws differ? What rights do the citizens have?
- How do the period-appropriate technologies produce evidence? Does the getaway horse have an identifiable horseshoe?
- How do social and cultural pressures affect access to resources? Does the peasant victim hold a piece of fabric so expensive that she's either a thief or her assailant is of a higher class? What weapons, tools, or disguises are affordable and available to characters?
- How do your characters measure time, distance, and other standardized scales?
- How can the relevant authority figures maintain scene security without crime scene tape?

Paranormal

In a supernatural world, the rules of your investigators are established during your worldbuilding.

Supernatural factors can make for fascinating crime scenes because worldbuilding moves the goalposts: bodies can rise from the dead after dying, investigators may be able to read minds, and villains may be able to literally enter a locked room or kill with a thought.

- Are the cops aware of the paranormal? What about the population? What legislation exists to govern paranormal activity?
- How do supernatural beings police themselves (or not)? How do humans and supernatural creatures interface and interact?
- Do they have paranormal technicians like claw mark experts or vampire odontologists in the way we have blood spatter analysts?
- Does a shifter's fur cause confusion at the scene? Do vampires leave fingerprints if they don't sweat?
- What slang exists to describe paranormal activity and communities? Who knows these terms and when are they used?
- If the world is magical, what residue do spells leave that can be collected at the scene?

Science Fiction

In a world ruled by technology, the crime scene can change dramatically. Let the *science* and philosophical questions raised by your invented world drive your investigations. Rather than letting tech solve all your problems, consider ways that all that advanced gadgetry creates problems and dilemmas for your characters.

- What sort of equipment does your world have that makes mine look ancient? Do hologram projectors play out scene reconstruction theories like movies?
- Is DNA outdated? What other types of identifiers have been discovered and developed?
- How is data gathered, stored, and obtained? How much oversight or lawlessness drives this civilization?
- What has value in this world? What is worth stealing, damaging, or destroying? How would criminals gain access?
- Using this world's technology, what is the simplest way for your character to injure or kill someone? The safest? The most certain?
- Do different lasers create different blast patterns? What sort of tracks do hover craft leave behind?
- If cross-contamination is a problem now, think of how exponentially more complicated it can get if the secondary scenes are in different time periods.
- What sort of "prime directive" would time cops have to follow?

Cracking the Cozy Mystery

How do you add realism to a story when the unassuming housewife or eager hobbyist does the detecting? How does an Average Jane or Joe gain access to the evidence needed to build a case?

From Jessica Fletcher to Nancy Drew to Scooby-Doo, the nosey amateur snoop has prowled through crime fiction since its Golden Age. Cozy mysteries, also called "cozies," tend to focus on the puzzle and the solution over the commission of the crime itself, and so do not necessarily linger on violence or pathology. These stories often involve novice meddlers who solve the crime just ahead of the police. The location tends to be remote, the circle of suspects stays small, and the finale normally involves laying out all of the clues in front of the entire cast to elicit a confession.

The entire purpose of a cozy is a fun read. The whodunit is the star and the relatability of the protagonist is the hook. So wouldn't all of the rules and regulations provided in this book just bog this entire genre down? The answer is yes. And no. And maybe. Cozies invariably require a hefty suspension of disbelief in all cases, as our next door neighbors aren't typically solving crimes, so you, the author, need to decide what realistic rules fit for your story, and which don't.

Since most evidence is found at crime scenes, cozy

writers have to find ways to get their curious meddlers onsite and in the mix. As you now know, crime
scenes are cordoned off and only people approved by
the lead investigator are let in. Some writers address
this by having their sleuth working with the police.
Dorothy L. Sayers had the police continually turn to
Lord Peter Wimsey based on his social position and
fascination with crime detecting. Sir Arthur Conan
Doyle and Agatha Christie sometimes had their police
consult private detectives Sherlock Holmes and
Hercule Poirot, respectively.

If the cozy's protagonist proceeds without the
police's blessing, then she must get to the scene before
the police arrive. This is why the protagonist often
finds the body herself in cozy mysteries. She may
have some sort of connection to the murder scene that
puts her there naturally. In Joanne Fluke's Hannah
Swensen series, the eponymous baker finds bodies
behind her own shop, in a competing bakery's
kitchen, and at a Christmas tree lot where she is
delivering cookies. Agatha Christie often has Jane
Marple visiting wealthy friends or relatives, to situate
her near the eventual murder. Finding an occupation
or hobby that gives the protagonist her own access
helps to work around the strict rules of police procedurals.

> **FUN FACT:** Agatha Christie found great success with her private detective, Hercule Poirot, mysteries, but much preferred writing her sleuthing busybody, Miss Marple.

Because the cozy sleuth has limited access, every piece of evidence tends to be significant and suspect interviews may feature more than strict forensics. Her role in these stories is to assemble the puzzle pieces, and she just doesn't have the training or official support to deal with excessive or unrelated evidence. Most of this important evidence is either overlooked by the police or considered inconsequential, but in the main character's eyes, makes a vital link in the solution's chain. For cozy cases it's always the *who* that matters, more than how they *dunnit*.

To follow the realistic rules of evidence described in this book, the protagonist in a cozy can simply turn the evidence she's found over to the police. She doesn't need the physical smoking gun as long as she knows it exists. In general, the climax of these stories is not a mountain of hard evidence at trial, but rather the main character building an incriminating narrative out of the meaningful puzzle pieces collected from the scene and the suspects in its perimeter. Almost always, a confession sinks the suspect here because the crime (and its scene) stay personal.

Quick References

As a means of helping to keep everything we covered

in this book accessible, I'm providing several tables for easy reference.

Building Your Crime Scene Checklist

In this chart I hope to help you map out your crime scene and outline its specifics. Every decision can help guide the actions the investigators take there.

CONSIDERATIONS WHEN BUILDING YOUR CRIME SCENE			
INDOORS		**OUTDOORS**	
CLOSED? – Residence/Room/Office		URBAN? – Neighborhood/Alley/Parking Lot	
OPEN? – Warehouse/Garage/Hangar		RURAL? – Back Road/Field/Woods/Stream	
SAFETY? - Occupants/Condition of Building		FEATURES? - Vegetation/Clutter/Equipment	
AMOUNT OF USED/FREE SPACE?		ANIMAL ACTIVITY?	
DEGREE OF CLEANLINESS/TIDINESS?		ACCESS & LANDSCAPE TYPE?	
TIME		**ENVIRONMENT**	
Season _____		Temperature _____	
Hour _____		Humidity _____	
Light ◁━━━━━━━━━▷ Dark		Weather? – Rain/Fog/Snow/Hail/Heat/Wind	
TERRAIN	**BIOHAZARDS**	**STAGING**	**MULTIPLE SCENES**
Obstacles?	Blood / Pathogens?	Contradictions?	Miscommunication?
Incline?	Disease?	Moved evidence?	Cross-contamination?
Refuse/Leaves?	Toxins?	Missing evidence?	Lack of personnel?
Water?	Radioactivity?	Planted evidence?	Lack of resources?

Figure 17: Considerations When Building Your Crime Scene

People at Your Crime Scene

Always remember who is at your scene and what their roles are. Are they in the way? Do they significantly change the scene? How do they affect your protagonist?

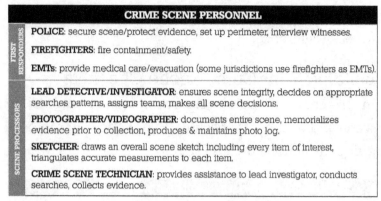

CRIME SCENE PERSONNEL	
FIRST RESPONDERS	**POLICE**: secure scene/protect evidence, set up perimeter, interview witnesses.
	FIREFIGHTERS: fire containment/safety.
	EMTs: provide medical care/evacuation (some jurisdictions use firefighters as EMTs).
SCENE PROCESSORS	**LEAD DETECTIVE/INVESTIGATOR**: ensures scene integrity, decides on appropriate searches patterns, assigns teams, makes all scene decisions.
	PHOTOGRAPHER/VIDEOGRAPHER: documents entire scene, memorializes evidence prior to collection, produces & maintains photo log.
	SKETCHER: draws an overall scene sketch including every item of interest, triangulates accurate measurements to each item.
	CRIME SCENE TECHNICIAN: provides assistance to lead investigator, conducts searches, collects evidence.

Figure 18: Crime Scene Personnel

Types of Search Patterns

This is a quick review of the types of crime scene search patterns. Your story may not need to be so specific, but considering what pattern is used in what type of scene might help you consider different complications or actions.

SEARCH PATTERNS		
LINE	Covers a massive area. Requires a LOT of personnel. Everyone moves in one direction.	
SPIRAL	Covers a large area. Start at outer circle and slowly spiral inward until entire area is covered.	
LANE	Can be indoor or outdoor. Searches up a lane and down a lane until area is covered.	
GRID	Can be indoor or outdoor. Searches up a lane and down a lane until area is covered. Then does a lane right and a lane left until area is covered again.	
ZONE	(*aka Quadrant*) Mostly used indoors or in well-defined outdoor areas. Each quadrant is assigned to a different searcher/team.	

Figure 19: Crime Scene Search Patterns

Types of Specialized Evidence Collection Equipment

We did not cover types of evidence to any great extent. The purpose of this book is to focus on the crime scene itself and how to process it. Including all the types of evidence would take us too far off the target topic. I will discuss each type of evidence and how it is collected in its own book. However, to help with your story, I'm providing a quick list of specific evidence and the specialized equipment needed in the crime scene kit.

SPECIALIZED EVIDENCE COLLECTION EQUIPMENT	
IMPRESSIONS	**FINGERPRINTS:** Powder, duster, and lifter (Lifters are typically tape or gels.)
	WET FINGERPRINTS: Small Particle Reagent (SPR) is a solution that sticks to the fatty acids in fingerprints, allowing for lifting in wet/rainy conditions.
	TOOL MARKS: Mikrosil is a silicone putty mixture that hardens to keep its shape within a tool mark. Unique features found within the tool mark can be matched to the same features on the exact tool that created the mark.
	FOOTPRINTS/TIRE MARKS: Dental stone or plaster mix creates a hardened cast of the print which can identify the shoe or tire that made it.
TRACE EVIDENCE	**GUNSHOT RESIDUE:** Solution that reacts to barium and antimony, which is a strong indication that the swabbed hand recently fired a gun.
	BLOOD DETECTORS: Many chemical solutions can be used to detect blood that is wiped up/not visible: Luminol, Hungarian Red, Cobalt Blue, and others.
	ALTERNATE LIGHT SOURCE: An ALS has two uses: changing the light's direction to create shadows, making dust prints, hair, fibers, etc. more visible, or changing the light wavelength, causing some fibers and body fluids to glow.

Figure 20: Specialized Evidence Collection Equipment

Closing Thoughts

"Writing is possibly an art, but crime writing is definitely a craft." – Ashwin Sanghi

You now have all the knowledge you need to create a compelling crime scene. There may seem to be a lot to consider, but it can all be summed up rather simply:

- The purpose of a crime scene is to protect, identify, and preserve evidence that proves or disproves an allegation.
- Crime scenes (in America) must follow the rules for searches set up by the Constitution and US laws.
- First responders take precedence over any investigative action. Human life and safety outweigh even the strongest evidence.
- One person, the lead investigator, takes charge at the scene and makes the decisions, including how to deal with various crime scene complexities.
- Scene integrity and scene security often dictate the success of crime scene processing.
- The type of scene can affect the type of search pattern conducted.
- The investigator must let the scene tell the story and not force it to support a predetermined conclusion, because it can be made to do so.

Finally, as with every forensic topic I teach, let me stress again that you must *solve your crime before you commit it*! Knowing how your protagonist resolves everything will only aid you in adding complications earlier in the story. Having to make up a solution at the last minute is an easy way to torpedo all of the work you put into the book previously.

You should never be nervous about writing crime or its investigation in your stories. You are able to write a *killer* scene, even when the scene of your book is the scene of the crime.

Glossary

Aperture – For photography, this is the size of the opening in the lens, which determines how much light will be captured. Measured in f-stops.

Bracketing – A photography technique that takes several photos of the same subject, but adjusts the f-stop for each one. This increases and decreases the amount of light for each of the photos, resulting in a range from overexposed to underexposed photographs. The purpose is to achieve a photo that is perfectly lit.

Chalk Outline – An outdated crime scene investigatory technique that memorialized a body's position after its removal from the scene. Today, crime scene sketches and photography fulfill its original purpose.

Close-Up Shot – A photograph taken at extreme close range that only captures the evidence of interest.

Consent – A legal search exception wherein an American citizen waives his or her Fourth Amendment protections against search and seizure. This waiving of their rights allows law enforcement to enter and search areas that would otherwise be protected as private. A consent can be limited to specific areas and may be revoked any time the person giving the consent chooses to.

Coroner – A county-level elected official whose primary responsibility is to investigate unnatural deaths within that county; not necessarily a doctor.

Crime – An act prohibited and punishable by law.

Crime Scene – Any location where any type of evidence may exist that is associated with a crime.

Crime Scene Cleaners – Privately owned businesses that clean-up and sterilize crime scenes after law enforcement has released them.

Crime Scene Integrity – For crime scenes, most often simply referred to as **Scene Integrity**.

Crime Scene Investigators – Law enforcement officials specially trained in overall or specific evidence collection at crime scenes.

Crime Scene Kit – A duffle bag or bin of necessary items used by a responding law enforcement official at crime scenes. The requirements for kits can vary from agency to agency, but typically contain evidence collection materials (bags, jars, labels, markers), flashlights, pens, pads of paper, agency forms, and personal protective equipment.

Crime Scene Security – For crime scenes, most often simply referred to as **Scene Security**.

Crime Scene Sketch – A hand-drawn representation of the crime scene, created on-site, that includes significant items (such as evidence), measurements, and directions.

Crime Scene Tape – Law enforcement ribbon, often brightly colored, that establishes a crime scene's perimeter, creating a boundary to keep unauthorized persons off the scene.

Cross-contamination – The transfer of evidence between scenes or onto objects not previously containing that evidence, which creates a false link between the objects.

CSIs – Crime Scene Investigators.

Curtilage – The area of land that surrounds a dwelling, which is considered private and protected against search and seizure.

Death Scene – A crime scene with a dead body on it. Actual jargon used by anyone on the scene.

Depth of Field – The distinct area within a photograph that appears in sharp focus.

Dive Team – For crime scenes, the squad of law enforcement personnel trained in underwater search and seizure.

Documentary Evidence – A category of evidence that is informational in nature. The data on a tax return, for example, is what's important, not the sheet of paper itself. So the tax return is documentary evidence.

Emergency Crime Scene – A crime scene created prior to the initiation of an investigation. These scenes are often reported during an emergency and are established by first responders.

Entry/Exit Point – A specific, manned location at the perimeter of a crime scene that is the single place everyone will have to pass through to get on or off the scene. This produces a measure of control and limits who can come onto the scene.

Entry/Exit Log – A record maintained at the entry/exit point that lists everyone coming onto the scene and their purpose.

Evidence – Anything that either proves or disproves how a crime was committed and/or who participated in it.

Evidence Log – The official list of all evidence collected at a scene. At a minimum, the evidence log contains a sequential number for each piece of evidence and a brief evidence description. Some logs may be more detailed in the descriptions and include the location the evidence was seized from and the seizing agent.

Evidence Markers – Anything used by investigators to disclose the location of each piece of evidence so they can come back to collect it later. Typically, evidence markers are brightly colored, numbered A-frames.

Evidence Tag – The document attached to each piece of evidence that lists the date, seizing agent's name, location of the evidence, evidence log number, and detailed description of the evidence itself. Often the evidence tag also includes the chain of custody for the evidence.

Evidence Triangle – The philosophy behind collecting evidence. The evidence becomes links between the scene and the suspect, the suspect and the victim and/or the victim and the scene.

Exclusionary Rule – The legal doctrine that establishes any evidence collected during an illegal search is inadmissible at trial.

Expectation of Privacy – Established by the Fourth Amendment to the US Constitution, no governmental official may search an area where reasonable privacy exists.

Exploded View Sketch – A sketching method that allows depicting evidence found on walls. In addition to the bird's-eye view of the floor, each wall of the room is also drawn, flattened out on each side.

Exposure – The darkness or lightness of a photograph. Underexposed photos are dark while overexposed images have too much light to accurately depict their subjects. Digital photography has greatly reduced either risk.

F-stop – In photography, the measurement for apertures. The smaller the f-stop, the more light that is allowed on the sensor.

False Scene – Crime scenes that have been staged in an attempt to misdirect investigators.

Federal Agency – A law enforcement entity that has authority under federal jurisdiction. Many federal agencies' jurisdictions are determined by case type. They are tasked with enforcing the laws within their jurisdictional limitations and conducting criminal investigations. They have a nationwide mandate.

Federal Jurisdiction – A legal authorization determined by geography. This level applies to federal agencies and extends nationwide.

Final Sketch – A careful reproduction of the crime scene sketch, drawn to scale and detailed. This version of the crime scene sketch is created after the scene has been released, and is suitable for court.

First Responders – An emergency service unit sent to answer an urgent distress call. First responders are made up of the police, firefighters, and Emergency Medical Technicians (EMTs). The first responsibility is the protection of life and property, followed by the preservation of the scene for the arrival of investigators.

Framing – Intentionally incriminating an innocent person through the use of false evidence or information.

Fruit of the Poisonous Tree – The legal doctrine that goes beyond the Exclusionary Rule by establishing that any evidence obtained later in the investigation from information gained as the result of an illegal search is inadmissible at trial.

Global Shots – Crime scene photographs that capture the entire area as it appears to someone approaching the scene on foot.

Inner Perimeter – In large enough crime scenes, this is a second boundary set up within the outer perimeter that surrounds the target scene. By establishing an inner perimeter, an area is created for a command post, a media box, and a set-up/break space for investigators while protecting the search area.

ISO – A camera's sensitivity to light. An ISO of 100 is considered low and works well when a lot of light is present, such as in daylight. A much higher ISO, such as 3200, means the camera is extremely sensitive to light and can take better photos in darker settings.

Jurisdiction – A legal endorsement that assigns authority. For crime scenes, jurisdiction determines which agency will run the case, which in itself determines who is going to be at the scene. Sometimes jurisdiction depends on geographical territory, sometimes by the agency, and sometimes by the type of crime.

Known Point – A fixed spot that will not easily change over time from which to make a measurement, such as a corner of a room or a tree trunk. Known points are essential for placing evidence back in its exact location during crime reconstructions.

Line Tender – A member of a crime scene dive team who remains on the surface and whose job is to continuously monitor the tether of his or her assigned diver.

Linkage Theory – The idea of how evidence can establish connections, often between a suspect and victim or between a person and a location.

Local Jurisdiction – A legal authorization determined by geography. This level applies to police departments and sheriff's offices and limits their law enforcement duties to villages, towns, cities, and counties.

Locard's Exchange Principle – A theory from Edmund Locard, who suggested that whenever two objects come into contact, an exchange occurs. For crime scenes, the theory explains that part of the suspect is always left behind at the scene, and part of the scene is always taken away with the suspect.

Locard's Theory of Exchange – An acceptable synonym for **Locard's Exchange Principle**.

Locard's Theory of Interchange – An acceptable synonym for **Locard's Exchange Principle**.

Mapping – Adding measurements to a sketch.

Medical Examiner – A hired forensic pathologist (doctor) whose primary responsibility is to investigate unnatural deaths within a defined geographical area. Medical examiners replace coroners in specific regions.

Mid-Range Shot – A photograph taken to show the evidence of interest and its position in the room as well its proximity to close-by items. It is a shot from which the evidence can be identified, but is not focused only on the evidence.

Outer Perimeter – The main boundary of a crime scene that surrounds the entire area. Primarily marked with crime scene tape, the purpose of the outer perimeter is to provide scene security by preventing any unauthorized persons access to the scene, thereby protecting scene integrity.

Overall Shot – A photograph taken to show as much of the environment around the evidence of interest as possible. If indoors it could be an entire room taken from the doorway. If outdoors, it's as wide a shot as possible. The evidence may not necessarily be identified in this shot, but it establishes the entire surroundings of the evidence.

Overexposed Photograph – Images that have too much light to accurately depict their subjects.

Painting with Light – A flash photography technique used in dark, large areas, such as an outdoor scene at night. For crime scenes, this technique will produce a picture showing the scene completely lit up, without shadow or poor visibility.

Perishable Evidence – Evidence that has the potential of changing over time, either physically by natural degradation, or geographically if routine crime scene processing procedures could result in moving its placement within the scene.

Personal Protective Equipment – Any of a variety of outer layer disposable clothing intended to create a barrier between potential pathogens and the person working in or around blood or other possible contagions. Appropriate PPE can be any or all of the following: latex gloves, shoe booties, sleeves, goggles, aprons, masks, and full bio-hazard suits.

Photo Log – A sequentially numbered list that describes each picture at the time it was taken, including, at a minimum, the date of the photo, where the photo was taken, and a description of what the photographer was attempting to capture.

Photo Scale – An acceptable synonym for **Photomacrographic Scale**.

Photomacrograph – A photograph that depicts the subject accurately, to scale.

Photomacrographic Scale – The specialized ruler used in crime scene photography to show size, orientation, and sometimes correct color of the photo's target.

Physical Evidence – A category of evidence that is anything not considered testimonial or documentary evidence. Any evidence that an investigator can physically hold, so not verbal or informational data.

PI – Private Investigator.

Plain View – A legal search exception that allows law enforcement to enter an area otherwise protected against search and seizure by the Fourth Amendment. As long as the officers are legally allowed to be in the spot they're occupying, if something illegal is in obvious sight, they may enter that protected area without getting a search warrant.

Police Department – A law enforcement agency that has authority under local jurisdiction. They are tasked with maintaining order, preventing and detecting crime, and enforcing the laws. They work in villages, towns, and cities.

PPE – Personal Protective Equipment.

Primary Scene – The first crime scene investigators respond to in their investigation. Any subsequent crime scene is referred to as a **secondary scene**.

Private Detective – An acceptable synonym for **Private Investigator**.

Private Eye – An acceptable synonym for **Private**

Investigator.

Private Investigator – A non-government, licensed individual hired to investigate a crime, surveille a targeted person, or make other such inquiries.

Probable Cause – A legal requirement specified in the Fourth Amendment to the US Constitution that limits law enforcement searches. Probable cause requires specific, reliable, current information that strongly suggests evidence is in the area to be searched.

Processing – For crime scenes, the methodical operation of searching a scene and seizing any evidence found there.

Reasonable – A legal standard that is set based on what a prudent, informed person would likely expect or how that person would likely act given different circumstance.

Rough Sketch – The original crime scene sketch drawn at the scene. Often not to scale and basic, this sketch is used to create a professional looking **final sketch** at a later date.

Routine Crime Scene – A crime scene that is initiated by investigators based off of their active casework and their own development of leads that demonstrate evidence exists at a specific location. This is differentiated from **emergency crime scenes**, which are initiated based on reported circumstances.

Scale – An acceptable synonym for **Photomacro-graphic Scale**. Actual jargon used by anyone conducting crime scene photography.

Scene Integrity – Several procedures used to protect the crime scene from alteration. Perimeter tape, a single pathway, and limiting who can enter the scene all work to keep the scene in pristine condition, while guarding against cross-contamination.

Scene Security – Officers make sure all witnesses, potential suspects, and victims are moved off of the scene and then establish a perimeter to prevent anyone from entering the scene without permission.

Secondary Scene – Any crime scene established after the first crime scene of an investigation (called the **primary scene**).

Sheriff's Office – A law enforcement agency that has authority under local jurisdiction. This is an elected position and the office is tasked with policing unin-corporated areas, maintaining county jails, and enforcing the laws. They work in counties.

Shutter Speed – In photography, how long the shutter stays open, meaning how long a camera's sensor is exposed to light.

Specialist – An expert trained in a specific field.

Staging – A purposeful act to alter a crime scene by adding, removing, or moving evidence with the explicit intention of misdirecting an investigation.

State Jurisdiction – A legal authorization determined by geography. This level applies to state police forces and limits their law enforcement investigations to within their own state.

State Police – A law enforcement agency that has authority under state jurisdiction. They are tasked with enforcing the laws and conducting criminal investigations. They are limited to working within their own state.

State Trooper – An acceptable synonym for **State Police**.

Target Scene – The primary area of the crime scene that requires a search for evidence.

Testimonial Evidence – A category of evidence that is verbal in nature. Informational evidence obtained during an interview.

Tether – A physical line that connects a diver to the surface. For underwater crime scenes, all divers are required to wear tethers because they often work in dangerous currents or areas of low-to-no visibility.

Transient Evidence – For crime scenes, an acceptable synonym for **Perishable Evidence**.

Triangulation – A technique used in crime scene sketching that provides accuracy for an item's specific location. This method uses two measurements for every item originating from fixed known points.

Underexposed Photograph – Images that have too little light to accurately depict their subjects.

Warrant – A legal authorization granting specific permissions to a government official. A search warrant authorized law enforcement agents to enter an area otherwise protected by the US Constitution. An arrest warrant authorizes officers to place an American citizen under arrest.

Writ – A formal document from the government or legal representative directing an official to complete or refrain from a specific act. A search warrant is a type of writ.

Bibliography

- *Advanced Crime Scene Photography (2nd Edition)* by Christopher D. Duncan (January 15, 2015)
- *Crime Scene Investigation and Reconstruction (3rd Edition)* by Robert R. Ogle Jr.(January 14, 2011)
- *Crime Scene Photography (3rd Edition)* by Edward M. Robinson (August 15, 2016)
- *Criminalistics: An Introduction to Forensic Science (10th Edition)* by Richard Saferstein (January 13, 2010)
- *Henry Lee's Crime Scene Handbook* by Henry C. Lee and Timothy Palmbach (July 25, 2001)
- *Practical Crime Scene Analysis and Reconstruction* by Ross M. Gardner and Tom Bevel (June 26, 2009)

Federal Material
US Constitution

Federal Court Rules
Federal Rules of Criminal Procedure
Federal Rules of Evidence

Index

About the Author

Geoff Symon is a twenty-year Federal Forensic Investigator and Polygraph Examiner. His participation in high-profile cases includes the attacks on September 11, 2001, the War in Iraq, the Space Shuttle Columbia explosion, the 2002 bombings in Bali and the Chandra Levy investigation, among countless other cases.

He has direct, first-hand experience investigating cases including murder (of all types), suicide, arson, kidnapping, bombings, sexual assault, child exploitation, theft and financial crimes. He has specified and certified training in the collection and preservation of evidence, blood spatter analysis, autopsies and laboratory techniques.

He has taught undergraduate and graduate-level college courses in forensics, including Basic Forensics, Crime Scene Processing and Crimes Against Children at the George Washington University (DC) and Marymount University (MD).

You can find him at GeoffSymon.com, Geoff Symon on Facebook and @geoffsymon on Twitter.

Thanks for spending some time with me exploring forensics. I hope you enjoyed this book and found it helpful in fleshing out the crime/investigations in your fiction. If so, please consider leaving a review at Amazon.com, Goodreads.com or any other site where you have posting privileges.

Visit forensicsforfiction.com for the latest updates and information about the other books in this series.

Geoff